YOUR CHILD'S GREATNESS

A PARENT'S GUIDE TO RAISING CHILDREN WITHOUT IMPOSTOR SYNDROME

Lisa Orbé-Austin, PhD
Richard Orbé-Austin, PhD

Published by:
Ulysses Press
PO Box 3440
Berkeley, CA 94703
www.ulyssespress.com

ISBN: 978-1-64604-769-7
Library of Congress Control Number: 2024944971

Printed in Canada
10 9 8 7 6 5 4 3 2 1

Acquisitions editor: Kierra Sondereker
Managing editor: Claire Chun
Project editor: Renee Rutledge
Proofreader: Sherian Brown
Cover design: Ashley Prine
Artwork: cover © Daniela Andrea Guasti/shutterstock.com; paint splatters © QuirkCraft Studio/shutterstock.com; pages 3 and 74 © Kiyan Fox
Interior design and production: Winnie Liu

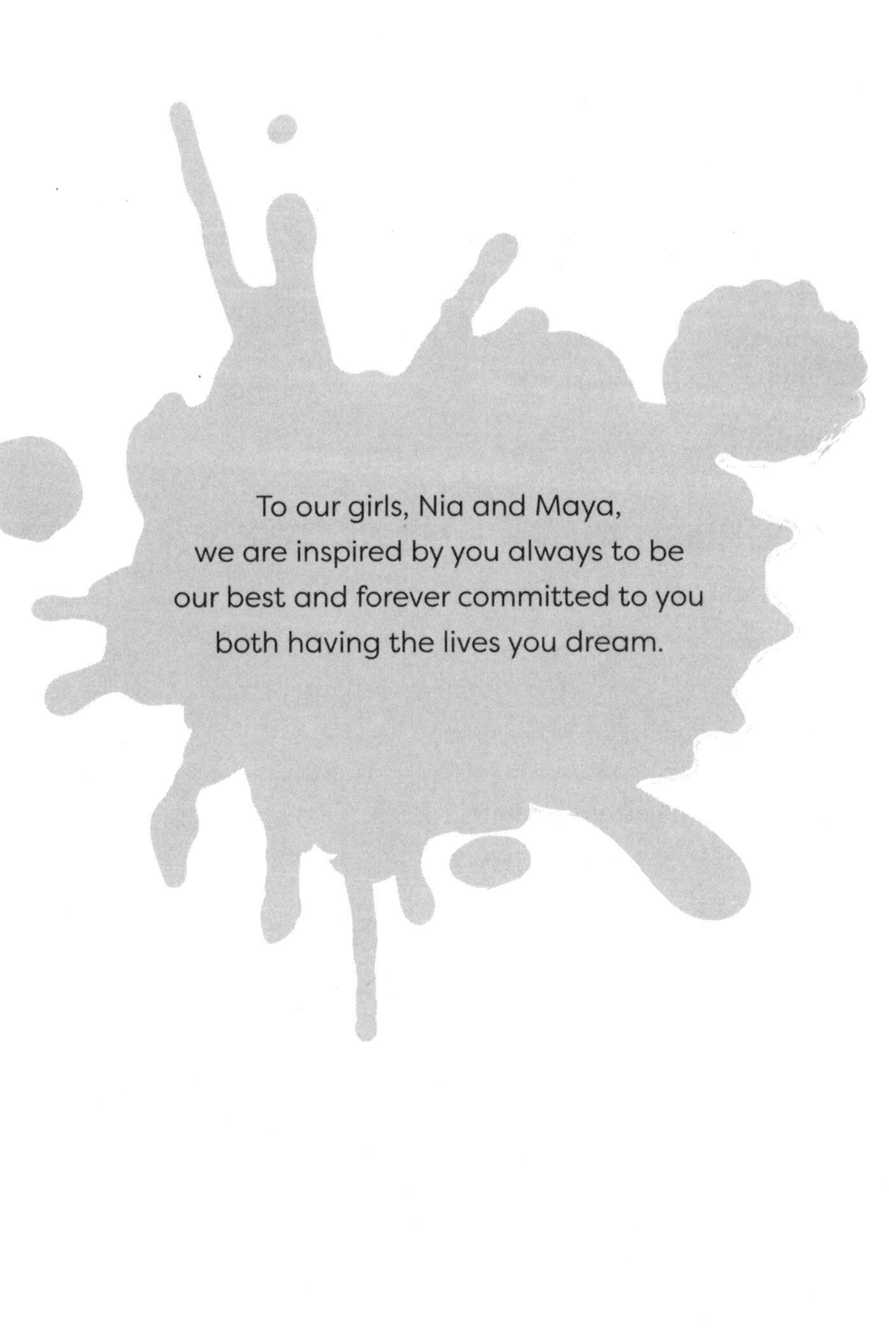

To our girls, Nia and Maya,
we are inspired by you always to be
our best and forever committed to you
both having the lives you dream.

CONTENTS

FOREWORD

I met the Orbé-Austins about seven years ago at the Peter Westbrook Foundation. I was still competing as an Olympic fencer when we met on the verge of my exit from competitive sport. I had a deteriorating "eighty-year-old hip," as my doctor described it. I was twenty-seven years old at the time. I think it is fair to say I was a hard worker.

The Orbé-Austins and I have kept in close touch throughout all of my seasons—my fencing retirement, being a coach of their two daughters, legislative advocacy with the City of New York, career exploration, social entrepreneurship, nonprofit leadership, and now in my new role as Mommy.

When Dr. Lisa asked me to write this foreword, I was completely stunned, flattered, and so pleased. The request coincided with one of the most joyful but chaotic periods in my life, a coming-of-age period for a late bloomer, if you may.

There is so much uncertainty during the immediate period after Baby is born. Life is forever changed. As the bearer of the baby, you will never be the same again—physically, mentally, and emotionally. And for many of us, the support system to care for the child is still forming, adjusting, and crystallizing, with many pending question marks and disappointed expectations.

It's important for me to lead with this here, as impostor syndrome not only has performance implications, but also very real personal implications. The skills in this book are a guidebook for all of us to not only fulfill our greatness, but also to protect ourselves from toxic relationships and harmful outcomes.

I've realized imposter syndrome at its core is about relationships. Through this text, I've deepened my understanding of unhealthy relationships and how this connected to my struggles as an athlete; how people-pleasing enabled some of my success, but also hindered my growth, and how my own regard for my value has been compromised at times.

Even though I achieved historic firsts during my Olympic athletic career, I never consistently defeated my imposter syndrome. I became the first American woman to win a Grand Prix in my discipline and was the first Black woman to individually medal at the Senior World Championships. I ranked as high as #5 in the world but still approached early-round matches with extreme caution and reserve. Reading through the automatic negative thoughts outlined by the authors triggered a number of toxic thinking patterns that overwhelmed me during competitions: predicting the future negatively, considering the worst case scenario when imagining outcomes, discounting my positives, and predicting a negative future. Negative thoughts that I actively tried to manage on competition days, and on my best days, rose above.

But managing sensations of doubt and unjustified inadequacy stretches far beyond the realm of professional achievements. It's a personal phenomenon that has to do with how your sense of self is built. It doesn't go away when you leave the arena of high-performance.

As you're reminded when reading through the informative pages to follow, relationships are the foundations of everything we do, and it's incredibly important to protect and strengthen your sense of self. Of course, performance is a focal point for many of us, but even performance is based on your relationship with yourself and how healthily you engage with others in the world.

As an athlete, my drive and success came from both positive and toxic, unsustainable sources: from wanting to appease my militant coach to wanting to win because it afforded me acceptance in an affluent, white dominated sport; from wanting to make Peter and the Foundation proud to being afraid of losing the glory and the thing that made me special.

Growing up in a single-family home, my mother's love and unwavering support provided the secure attachment for me to trust and find confidence in my power. My mother taught me to give my all and have fun. In anything I did, she allowed me total autonomy; she didn't push me to study, practice, or compete. Instead, I was the one who nagged my mother to take me to test prep, register me for competitions, or drive me to fencing. I was the captain of my ship. My mom managed the logistical obstacles and gave me unconditional love, allowing me to focus on my passions.

These interpersonal relationships, whether toxic or not, shaped my work ethic,

Willpower, and ability to be one of the best. I appreciate the Orbé-Austins for helping us make sense of the wild journey through the lens of parenthood.

In the context of a sport, these habits were not life impacting. Perhaps, they limited my consistency in achieving success—but it did not make or break my life.

When you leave sport and enter the real world, as I did in the last five years, these patterns of thinking have life-changing consequences. Without the awareness of self and your value, you are liable to let others take advantage of you, manipulate you, and assert their will in your life. For me, this book has reminded me that my own mind and voice are so capable, and I can't afford to drown them out while listening to everyone else's. Especially because others' intentions are not always as they seem.

Here is a guide to protect your mental health from undue, unsolicited, and unqualified influence. To arm both you and your child with skills of discernment, to battle complex relationships, including the one with yourself. Then, implement actionable skills and mindfulness exercises to ultimately achieve your greatness.

Reading through *Your Child's Greatness*, I came across nuggets of information not only to apply to my daughter's development, but more so for me. Perhaps as a parent, to deliver these important lessons, you will need to recognize your own limitations first.

—Nzingha Prescod,
two-time Olympian and World Champion

INTRODUCTION

Throughout the years that Richard and I (Lisa) have spoken to, trained, and taught people how to use the skills that are effective in reducing and eliminating impostor syndrome, one resounding question has come up time and time again: "When are you going to write an impostor syndrome book for parents?" It often comes from an individual who seems heart-struck at the possibility that they may have inadvertently reinforced ideas, behaviors, and principles that set impostor syndrome in motion for yet another generation.

I vividly remember one such conversation with an executive leader and mom of a college student. As I was heading out to catch my flight, she rushed to tell me that after the talk I had given to her leadership group, she had immediately called her son and apologized. She said that she had often called him "lazy" and was frustrated at all his constant issues at school, attributing them to his lack of effort. Until hearing my talk, she hadn't realized that he might be struggling with impostor syndrome. She recounted telling her son that they were going to do what it took to figure out what was going on with him and address it head-on.

I found myself tearing up at how a talk for executive leaders about how to overcome impostor syndrome could help a family come together and perhaps begin a journey of healing, seeing each other as whole and complicated people, and doing the work to support each other's true, and at the same time, ever-changing selves. It dawned on me at that moment that we needed to write this book.

Over the years, as we have watched our children grow up, we have seen just how many adults would benefit from this book, whether they are parents, coaches, caregivers, teachers, relatives, mentors of children, or just about anyone who is influential to children. While the influence of a parent or caregiver is incredibly important, in an age when children spend so much more time with other adults besides their parents—in school, caretaking, and extracurriculars—everyone needs a sense for how to set children in adaptive and healthy ways: to internalize their strengths and areas for development, learn to speak about themselves, set boundaries, navigate conflict, prevent codependent and narcissistic dynamics, learn self-care, and so much more to prevent the development of impostor syndrome.

Your Child's Greatness is meant to be a guide to the principles and skills that are critical in the development of healthy self-esteem in children, including an ability to develop an internal sense of validation and self; the skills to handle critical feedback with an aim toward growth; a focus on collaboration and building community around them; and a lack of fear around who they are, what they want, and the journey that they are on. We want to give you techniques and processes that can help you work with your child from the very beginning until they are independent (or interdependent) from you to continue to nurture trust in themselves because they have an honest and accurate viewpoint of who they are and the support they have around them.

In this book, we are going to take you through the 3 B's Model.

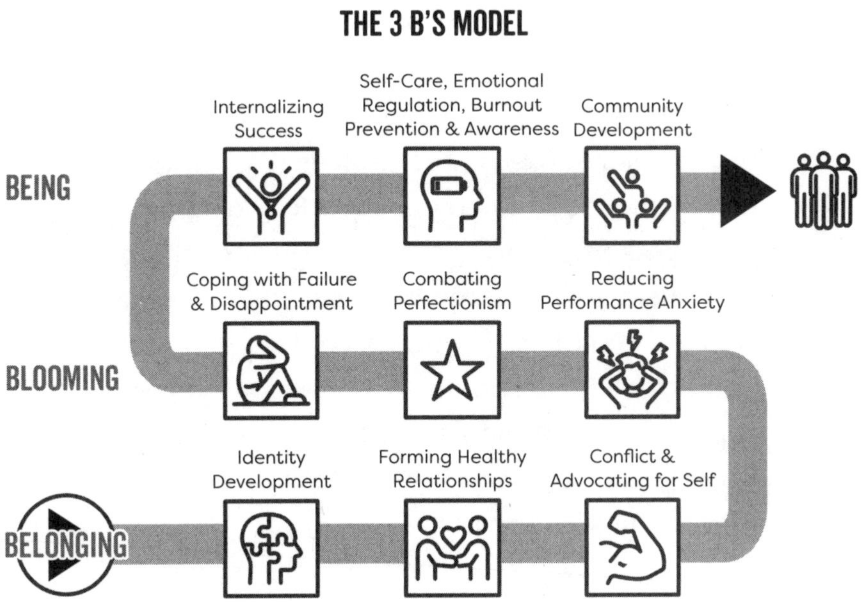

THE 3 B'S MODEL

BEING

Internalizing Success

Self-Care, Emotional Regulation, Burnout Prevention & Awareness

Community Development

BLOOMING

Coping with Failure & Disappointment

Combating Perfectionism

Reducing Performance Anxiety

BELONGING

Identity Development

Forming Healthy Relationships

Conflict & Advocating for Self

The first phase is Belonging. In this particular phase, we focus on important family and group dynamics that are critical to the healthy development of self. Here, we will center on foundational dynamics that are key to providing the initial template from which your child will develop other relationships, including romantic relationships, work relationships, and friendships. In these steps, we will explore family dynamics that can be problematic and ways in which to shift them to produce better results and safer environments for the family as a whole. We will also discuss how to help your child learn in a world that seems more fragmented, polarized, and isolated than ever; how to develop lasting relationships with others; how to deal with ruptures and conflict in relationships; and how to repair them productively when possible. Then, we will talk about how to support your child in understanding how to identify toxic relationships and when to let go of them.

In the second phase, we will cover Blooming. This work will be centered on internally focused growth that children need to develop a solid sense of themselves. We'll manage some common dilemmas that come up, especially as they contribute to impostor syndrome. This section will also teach you how to build skills to help your children deal with performance anxiety and help them to address it when it comes up. In addition, we will give you tips for attending to perfectionism in your child, including providing methodologies to approach perfectionism in a very different way so that it doesn't become limiting, constricting, confining, and alienating of others. Finally, we will discuss how to cope with failure in a healthy manner.

The final stage is Being. We will conclude by supporting your child with strategies and tools that will teach them how to internalize success to have an accurate perspective of their skills, strengths, and abilities. We'll discuss burnout and how to teach children from a young age to develop consistent and replenishing self-care habits. You will learn how to help children understand and utilize a self-care routine that is consistent and prioritized, even in our overscheduled, achievement-bound, and exhausted world. You will not only help your child gain the language and tools for this, but you will also model it, as children are more likely to do what they see rather than what they are told. Lastly, we will focus on teaching kids the skills to build healthy communities around them, which is crucial when impostor syndrome leaves you feeling alone and isolated. Community can be critical in building a resilient and protective group that rallies around you in difficult moments.

We look forward to this book being something that you can read and use throughout your child's development. We see it as a volume that you will return to repeatedly and hope you revisit certain chapters when you particularly need them and when they feel relevant. We hope this book ushers your child into an adulthood where they feel competent and confident yet always open to learning, making mistakes, and discovering new parts of themselves in a curious and ever-expanding pursuit to be all the greatness they and you can imagine.

Chapter One

DEVELOPING IDENTITY, SELF-WORTH, AND SELF-ESTEEM

Who am I? What are the values and beliefs that I think of as fundamental? What personal qualities do I value most in myself? How do I define success and fulfillment? How do I respond when faced with failure and setbacks? How do I feel about the person that I am becoming? Does that person change in different contexts? Developing a sense of self is not just important; it's essential to support when raising healthy children who will become healthy adults. Several aspects of identity development are critical for children, especially in avoiding the formation of impostor syndrome. The experience of impostor syndrome can make the sense of yourself temporal, fragile, and driven by external opinion, whether negative or positive. Many people who struggle with impostor syndrome grew up in environments that did not attend to the development of their own unique identity. This is often because caregivers were too engrossed in other things to be aware of the person developing before them. In trying to prevent impostor syndrome from happening, parents must consciously attend to their child's ability to build self-confidence and maintain a healthy sense of self.

People who experience impostor syndrome often have the following misconceptions:

- They are only valuable when they play certain roles (e.g., the superperson, the "good kid," the person who never says no).
- Praise and/or negative evaluation are fundamental to their sense of self.
- When they make mistakes or pursue things that are not of interest to others they value, they see themselves as unworthy and feel intense shame.
- In new situations, they are in search of who they are rather than possessing a steady and consistent sense of self.

Identity development can seem like a mysterious process that parents and caregivers have little to do with or have too much influence in. We encourage you to be the conscious stewards of this experience until your child can steward it for themselves. This does not mean forcing your child into a mold of what you may want but supporting their development with careful attention to how that influence could stifle them, make them insecure, or arrest that development. Your role is critical in the establishment of core values and beliefs, exposure to cultural traditions, modeling boundaries and expectations of people, helping them to understand their strengths and weaknesses, showing their worthiness when mistakes are made and failures happen, and most importantly, strengthening their relationship with you during this incredibly formative time.

IMPOSTOR SYNDROME AND IDENTITY

Impostor syndrome is largely set in motion in the early formative years by how a child relates to the adults in their world and how the adults relate to them. In this chapter, we will discuss some of the key principles that you will want to integrate into your parenting to ensure that your child builds a solid sense of identity that isn't so fragile that it is subject to the whims of others.

Inherent in impostor syndrome is an absent and highly influenced sense of self. The person is largely reliant on the opinions of others to evaluate who they are, what they want, and what they can do. They can feel like they are a fraud in part because their conception of what it means to be competent and capable is unrealistic and based purely on external validation, which is often not possible. Therefore, you can see that excessive approval and praise is not the route either because children can become reliant on it to understand who they are.

SELF-ESTEEM VS. SELF-WORTH

It's important to differentiate between the concepts of self-esteem and self-worth. Self-esteem is "confidence in yourself and a belief in your qualities and abilities."[1] It is how you feel

1 Cambridge Learner's Dictionary, "Self-Esteem," Cambridge University Press, https://dictionary.cambridge.org/us/dictionary/learner-english/self-esteem, accessed June 15, 2024.

about who you are, what you can do, and even what you can't do. Self-esteem is likely to fluctuate, and although we want to make sure that generally it is in a positive place, it may not always be, and that is completely adaptive and normal.

On the other hand, self-worth is "a sense of your own value as a human being."[2] This should not fluctuate. Your child should always feel like they have value as a human being and that their life is valuable, valued, and important. No matter what happens with their confidence, they should have self-worth, and this should always be supported by those around them, especially in the early years as it is developed. Eventually, the hope is that they establish an internalized self-worth and others will not need to support this as much over time.

THE INTERSECTION OF PARENTING AND IDENTITY DEVELOPMENT

Parenting styles profoundly impact identity development in children, and it's essential for parents to reflect on their own approaches. Understanding whether one's parenting style leans toward authoritarian, permissive, or authoritative can help identify the influences these styles have on a child's emerging identity:

- Authoritarian parenting exists when parents have high expectations for their child but don't tend to provide a lot of emotional support for this child. They exhibit a "my way

2 Merriam-Webster, "Self-Worth," https://www.merriam-webster.com/dictionary/self-worth, accessed June 15, 2024.

or the highway" attitude. This style is often correlated to children having issues with self-esteem, difficulty making decisions on their own, and having trouble with being autonomous, relying on others for feedback or validation.

- Permissive parenting, with high responsiveness but low demands, may result in a lack of boundaries and self-discipline.
- Authoritative parenting is a balance of high expectations and an ability to respond to a child's needs and unique circumstances with responsiveness. This style of parenting often fosters independence, self-regulation and co-regulation, and a positive self-concept.

Additionally, parents must consider their own experiences, including any trauma or unresolved issues from their upbringing, as these can unconsciously influence their parenting style. Without addressing and healing these traumas, there is a risk of replicating dysfunctional dynamics, perpetuating a cycle of negative identity development across generations.

As children mature, it becomes crucial for parents to differentiate between themselves and their children. This differentiation acknowledges that a child is a unique individual with their own thoughts, feelings, and future aspirations rather than being an extension of the parent. Recognizing and respecting this individuality helps promote a child's autonomy and self-identity. As children grow and eventually separate from their parents, this healthy differentiation supports their ability to navigate life independently. The role of the parent is multifaceted: to model positive behavior, to guide and support the child in becoming a unique individual, and to be vigilant of family dynamics that may hinder healthy identity development. Dysfunctional family patterns, if left unaddressed, can significantly impact a child's sense of self and their ability to form healthy relationships.

ATTACHMENT, PARENTING, AND THE DEVELOPMENT OF IMPOSTOR SYNDROME

Attachment and security are foundational elements in developing a child's identity and self-concept. When a child is securely attached to their caregivers because they can trust that they will show up for them consistently, be responsive to them, and provide them love and safety, they are more likely to develop better connections with others and themselves. When children feel securely attached, they are more likely to develop a positive self-concept and the confidence to explore their environment and take on challenges. Emotional safety is a vital part of this process and entails creating an environment where the expression of all emotions is safe and vulnerability is met with care and responsibility. This sense of security and validation fosters a resilient sense of self, reducing the likelihood of developing feelings of inadequacy and self-doubt and contributing to impostor syndrome later in life.

Unconditional love and acceptance play a vital role in a child's emotional development and self-esteem. When parents demonstrate affection and support unconditionally, children learn that they are valued for who they are rather than for their achievements or conformity to expectations. This acceptance is crucial for helping children internalize a sense of worthiness and belonging. In a nonjudgmental environment, children are encouraged to express their thoughts and feelings without fear of criticism or rejection. This promotes self-acceptance and authenticity, enabling children to develop a stable and positive self-identity, which serves as a buffer against the doubts and insecurities associated with impostor syndrome.

Persistent feelings of inadequacy and the fear of being exposed as a fraud can be traced back to childhood experiences of attachment and validation. Children who lack secure attachment and unconditional acceptance may grow up feeling that their worth is contingent upon their achievements or the approval of others. This conditional sense of worth can lead to chronic self-doubt and the belief that they are not genuinely competent, even in the face of success. Without a secure foundation of self-worth, these children may attribute their accomplishments to external factors such as luck or deception rather than their own abilities, fostering the feelings of fraudulence that define impostor syndrome.

Effective parenting practices emphasizing secure attachment and unconditional love can mitigate the risk of developing impostor syndrome. By consistently providing a nurturing and emotionally safe environment, parents help children build a strong, positive self-concept. Encouraging children to embrace their authentic selves, celebrate their unique strengths, and accept their imperfections fosters resilience and self-assurance. These children are more likely to grow into adults who trust in their own abilities and feel deserving of their successes. Ultimately, the intersection of attachment, parenting, and identity development highlights the profound influence of early relational experiences on lifelong psychological well-being.

THE VALUE OF COMMUNICATION AND OPEN DIALOGUE

Practicing active listening is foundational in fostering trust and making children feel understood and valued. Active listening involves giving your full attention, acknowledging your child's feelings, and responding thoughtfully without immediate judgment or interruption. When parents use this tool, a child is more likely to feel heard and seen, which can positively affect their self-worth. Active listening strengthens the relationship and attachment with your child and also gives them an allowance to fully express themselves without fear of punishment or retribution. As a result, children develop confidence in their own voice and thoughts, which is crucial for forming a positive self-concept and a strong sense of identity.

Encouraging open dialogue about identity, values, and personal experiences is another key aspect of helping children feel safe to articulate their thoughts and feelings, concerns and curiosities. When parents engage in such discussions, they provide children with the language and framework to explore complex aspects of their identity. These conversations help them understand and integrate various elements of their identity, such as their cultural background, personal values, and individual preferences. By discussing these topics openly, parents help children develop a coherent and resilient sense of self that is well-informed and reflective of their true nature.

ACTIVE LISTENING SKILLS

SKILL	DESCRIPTION
Paying Full Attention	Giving your child full and undivided attention, completely focusing on what they are saying while being mindful to avoid distractions.
Reflective Listening	Paraphrasing or summarizing what your child has said to show understanding and confirm accuracy.
Clarifying	Asking questions to ensure understanding of your child's message, and to clarify any ambiguous points.
Empathizing	Demonstrating understanding of your child's feelings; showing empathy and concern.
Nonverbal Cues	Using body language such as nodding, maintaining eye contact, and leaning forward to show attentiveness and engagement.
Giving Feedback	Providing thoughtful, constructive responses that acknowledge your child's points and contribution to the conversation.
Summarizing	Restating key points and ideas to confirm understanding and ensure the main message has been received accurately.
Avoiding Interruptions	Allowing your child to finish their thoughts without interrupting, ensuring they have a chance to express their complete message.

The practice of open communication and active listening goes beyond merely addressing immediate concerns; it shapes the long-term development of a child's identity. When children feel that their parents genuinely care about their opinions and experiences, they are more likely to internalize a sense of self-worth and self-acceptance.[3] This positive self-view is critical for navigating life's challenges and making autonomous decisions aligned with their values. Moreover, consistent communication and dialogue equip children with the skills to articulate their needs and boundaries effectively, fostering healthy relationships in the future. Ultimately, the value of communication and open dialogue in parenting cannot be overstated, as it lays the groundwork for children to develop into confident, self-aware individuals with a strong and positive identity.

THE DEVELOPMENT OF SELF-CONFIDENCE

"Confidence is the ability to see yourself as a flawed individual and still hold yourself in high regard."
—Terrence Real

Supporting the development of self-esteem and self-confidence in children means helping them explore the full range of who they are and being able to appreciate that in its current state. This doesn't mean that they don't have goals or want to improve; they most certainly do. It means that we do not teach our children to judge themselves by some future self or goal for themselves. We show and model how to appreciate their current self *and* still be able to have areas for improvement, goals, and aspirations. This *both-and* concept is such an important skill to illustrate as opposed to either-or. We are trying to teach them

3 María del Carmen Pérez-Fuentes, et al., "Parenting Practices, Life Satisfaction, and the Role of Self-Esteem in Adolescents," *International Journal of Environmental Research and Public Health* 16, no. 20 (2019): 4045, doi:10.3390/ijerph16204045.

not to dichotomize how they see themselves in the world. Life does not occur in the black and white; it mostly happens in the gray. Moving away from these concepts of black and white, good and bad, love and hate is very helpful, especially in the exploration of identity and the understanding of experience with greater nuance, description, and context. The richness of what happens in the depth of understanding of their experience is the most significant, with detail and exploration.

With impostor syndrome, there is always an ideal self that is unattainable, against which you will always be deficient in comparison. This concept is what often leaves individuals feeling inadequate, as if they are missing the mark. Help your child understand that goals are very helpful but achievement of those goals happens over time. Every incremental movement toward progress takes perseverance, skills, and abilities and should be honored, respected, and internalized. This allows a child to appreciate small developmental changes and growth over time rather than focusing on the end goal alone.

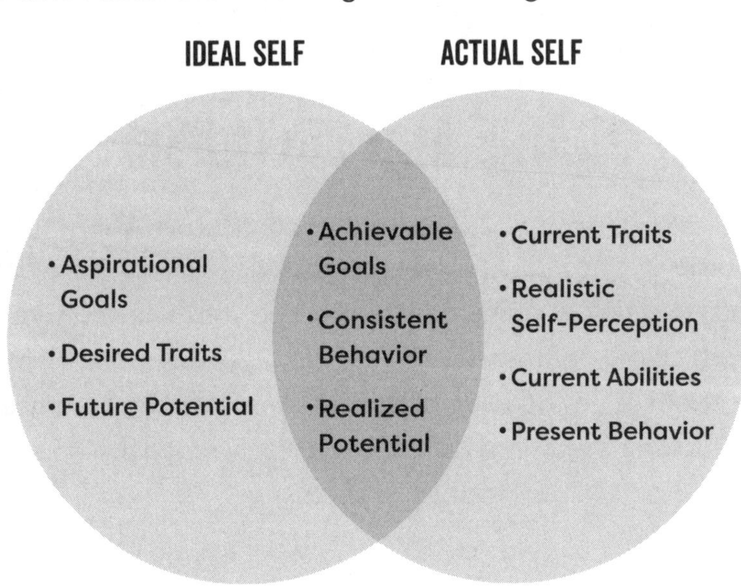

As a parent, it's important not to project an idealized version of your child onto them. For example, you might want your child to be a concert violinist, and this is the hope and expectation that you hold for them. As a result, if they are not progressing as a future concert violinist, their lack of progression might prevent you from noticing all the ways in which they are growing and building new skills at their pace, focusing instead on the issues with their practice, performance, and attending to their violin. This can leave a child centered on the ways they are lacking and not moving forward and unable to understand their effort and growth. With impostor syndrome, a hyperfocus tends to be placed on what's not happening, with little attention on the progress that has been made, especially around expectations from trusted others. It's okay to have expectations for your children, but how you deal with them not meeting those expectations becomes incredibly important. The same thing is true for how you model this for your children in your own behavior. You want to model that you can *both* appreciate where you are *and*, at the same time, appreciate how you can grow.

PRAISE AND CRITICISM

Praise and criticism are central features of the impostor syndrome cycle. Individuals with impostor syndrome were so reliant on external validation as children that they continue to seek praise to confirm they are on the right track. Criticism can make them hyperfocus on their mistakes and beat themselves up for making them. They often completely neglect any positive outcomes and fail to internalize them.

When you offer praise to your child, focus on the specific effort, behavior, or skill that they used to get to that moment of success, and not a general offering of praise. This helps in the development of a growth mindset. Additionally, offer praise for completed steps of the process along the way. Ensure that your child is taking in and internalizing their understanding of their contribution to their success (i.e., what skill, ability, or behavior led them to that success). This helps them to build a greater understanding of themselves and their strengths.

All kids need constructive feedback, but how you give that feedback is incredibly important to their development. Constructive feedback centers on the behavior that needs improvement and ways that they can improve it. As your child attempts correction, provide supportive encouragement and praise for the incremental work toward changing. You shouldn't save your recognition of change until after they have reached the desired outcome. Providing constructive feedback along with positive reinforcement (i.e., balanced feedback) helps children recognize areas for improvement while still feeling competent and valued.

It also becomes critical to process any kind of emotional dysregulation that occurs as a result of giving them constructive feedback. Hearing that you didn't perform as expected from someone you love can elicit feelings of fear and concern about that relationship and can provoke attachment anxiety. It's very important your child always know that they are loved and valued for who they are, even when you are giving them constructive feedback. You should never remove affection or attention when giving critical feedback. It sends the message that your love is conditional and only present when they do as you want them to. This is very dangerous and sets the foundations for impostor syndrome–the feeling that you are only worthy of attention, love, or support when doing what another person wants you to do. This feeling often underlies the people-pleasing component of the experience.

Teaching your child the growth mindset as early as you can passes on a valuable tool for them as they evaluate the meaning of intelligence, success, achievement, and capability. With a fixed mindset, you believe that you are who you are and that there is very little that you can do to change yourself. Possible opportunities are due to those preexisting and unchangeable capabilities. With the growth mindset, you believe that failure and mistake-making are a natural part of any learning experience. The better you are at making mistakes and recovering from them through a process of learning from them, the more capable you are of growing and getting better throughout your lifetime. The idea is that a moment will never exist when you don't make mistakes, no matter how expert you become, which is normal. Hypersensitivity from impostor syndrome can be traced to a fixed mindset belief.

RESILIENCE AND COPING SKILLS

Learning resilience and coping skills are critical to your child's healthy identity. Resilience is the ability to bounce back from adversity, tough times, and challenges, and coping is using strategies and skills to manage stress and difficulty. When parents both demonstrate and teach resilience to their child, they provide them with the tools needed to handle life's inevitable setbacks. Foundationally children need a family environment where they can express their feelings and experiences and address tough moments. Children should be encouraged to face challenges rather than be shielded from all discomfort, in order to develop problem-solving skills and confidence in their ability to overcome obstacles. Additionally, it is important to validate their feelings, and guide them through difficult situations, which reinforces the notion that they can manage and survive tough times.

Positive, adaptive, and healthy coping strategies often need to be taught. Kids can learn them from others or discover them on their own, but it is best when those around use and reinforce those techniques. Effective coping strategies can include activities such as deep breathing, meditation, exercise, emotional regulation, positive self-talk, and seeking support from others, all of which can help children address stress and maintain emotional balance. We will cover this in greater detail in the Performance Anxiety chapter.

Parents can foster these skills by modeling calm and constructive responses to their own stress and by actively teaching their children techniques for managing their emotions. Show your child how to understand that failure and setbacks are a part of life, not a shameful indication of something lacking within them. Through this process, children learn that they have the inner strength to handle challenges, which contributes to a positive self-concept and a stronger sense of identity. Ultimately, resilient children with effective coping mechanisms are better equipped to navigate the complexities of life, leading to healthier emotional and psychological development and a strong, adaptable sense of self.

SUPPORTING THE DEVELOPMENT OF AUTONOMY

Children with a healthy sense of autonomy exhibit greater independence and confidence, which are essential defenses against impostor syndrome. When you allow your child to navigate challenges independently in an age-appropriate and developmentally appropriate manner, you empower them to take ownership of their behaviors and choices. Express your belief in your child's decision-making and teach them that they are capable and trustworthy and can employ a methodology to solve the problems in front of them. They'll learn that they can tackle difficulties and find solutions, reinforcing their self-efficacy. Progressively increase the complexity of decisions your child is allowed to make to help them build confidence in their judgment and abilities. This growing sense of self-assurance and autonomous decision-making ability will become a vital component of their identity, making them less likely to experience the self-doubt, insecurity about their choices, and feelings of fraudulence that characterize impostor syndrome.

The importance of supporting autonomy extends beyond fostering immediate skills; it also impacts children's long-term development and their ability to internalize a positive self-concept and robust sense of self. This strong self-identity becomes a bulwark against external pressures and internal doubts. Children who have been encouraged to be autonomous are more likely to internalize their successes and view themselves as capable individuals, reducing the likelihood of attributing achievements to external factors like luck, someone helping them in ways that they did not deserve, or accidents. This internalization is key to preventing the chronic self-doubt and feelings of inadequacy that lead to impostor syndrome.

AUTONOMY IN CHILDHOOD EXAMPLES

ELEMENTARY SCHOOL

- Making their own school lunch
- Preparing their snacks
- Making their bed and tidying room
- Putting their own laundry away

MIDDLE SCHOOL

- Speaking directly to their teacher about an issue rather than have parents do it
- Taking responsibility for completing homework
- Organizing their own things
- Making simple meals

HIGH SCHOOL

- Earning money to purchase things they want and managing money in general (e.g., plan for savings, budgeting)
- Doing their own laundry, preparing meals, cleaning their rooms

- Independence; getting to do things with friends without supervision
- Being responsible for their own academic progress and being prepared for class

Additionally, autonomy helps children navigate the complexities of adult life with confidence and self-reliance. Autonomy combats potential experiences of codependence and the need to rely on others, which is so pervasive in impostor syndrome. We want to allow children, especially as they grow older, to make decisions and choices that are their own, even if that's not what we would have chosen for them. Allow your child to have their own life separate from yours, especially in early to late adolescence. When our children are young, we do make almost all decisions for them, but gradually, we want to relinquish the reins so that they can be their own person, which may be very different from who you are and what you expect them to be. Tolerating this and supporting their decisions become important parts of developing their autonomy.

Individuals with a sense of autonomy are better equipped to adapt to changing circumstances and to pursue their goals with determination.[4] They are more likely to take risks, embrace new opportunities, and recover from setbacks without succumbing to debilitating self-doubt. By fostering autonomy, parents provide their children with the tools necessary to build a strong, positive identity and a sense of self-worth that shields them

4 Joseph P. Allen et al., "Longitudinal Assessment of Autonomy and Relatedness in Adolescent-Family Interactions as Predictors of Adolescent Ego Development and Self-Esteem," *Child Development* 65, no. 1 (1994): 179–194, doi:10.1111/j.1467-8624.1994.tb00743.x.

from the negative effects of impostor syndrome. Ultimately, the development of autonomy is not just about immediate independence or complete separation from family, but about preparing children for a lifetime of confident, self-assured living.[5]

THE IMPORTANCE OF ROLE MODELING IN IDENTITY DEVELOPMENT

Role modeling is a fundamental aspect of parenting that significantly impacts a child's identity development and their sense of self. Children are in constant observation mode. They learn a lot more from what is done and the behavior that gets repeated than they do from being instructed to do something that no adult is also engaging in. In modeling positive behaviors and self-concept, you provide a powerful template for your children to emulate. This includes demonstrating self-respect, self-care, and resilience in the face of challenges. By observing your healthy ways of dealing with stress, failure, and success, your children internalize these behaviors, which contributes to a robust and positive sense of self. Role modeling is an essential tool to reinforce behavior and demonstrate its effectiveness in your own adult life.

Parents showcase their values and principles through their daily actions and decisions. When you consistently act in accordance with your values, such as with honesty, kindness, and

5 Chunhua Ma, Yongfeng Ma, and Youpeng Wang, "Parental Autonomy Support and Mental Health among Chinese Adolescents and Emerging Adults: The Mediating Role of Self-Esteem," *International Journal of Environmental Research and Public Health* 19, no. 21 (1994): 14029, https://doi.org/10.3390/ijerph192114029.

perseverance, you reinforce these traits in your children. This consistency helps them understand the importance of aligning their actions with their beliefs, fostering a sense of integrity and authenticity. As children witness you navigating life's complexities while staying true to your values, they learn to appreciate and adopt these principles in their own lives. For example, when you are having difficulty at work because you see that women are being treated poorly and your values are aligned around equity for women and you handle it by being active, starting an employee resource group (ERG), this shows agency in how you address situations and perhaps even apply for new jobs. This alignment is crucial for developing a coherent and stable identity, where children feel secure and confident in who they are because how to handle challenges to your values and principles is modeled for them in clear ways.

Parents can also be role models for self-awareness, growth, and improvement. When you openly acknowledge your mistakes, take responsibility, and show a commitment to personal growth, you teach your children the value of self-improvement and resilience. This transparency helps children understand that it is okay to be imperfect and that growth is a lifelong process. By witnessing your journey of self-discovery and improvement, your children are encouraged to embrace their own development with an open and positive mindset. They no longer see you as a perfect and unattainable model of what it means to be an adult.

IDENTIFYING LEARNING ISSUES EARLY

School and the educational realm are often the first places where performance can become an issue for those with impostor syndrome. In our work with clients over the years, we have seen a noticeable segment of those with impostor syndrome struggle with some kind of often undiagnosed learning issue(s) that they have had to either overcompensate for or build upon other strengths to minimize. This has often left them feeling incapable or unintelligent.

It is crucial to identify learning issues early in order to provide children with the appropriate support and resources, ensuring they reach their full potential and build adaptive skills and awareness. Neurodivergence and learning disabilities can affect how children process information, but they do not necessarily correlate with a lack of intelligence or potential for success. Recognizing these challenges early allows for educational approaches that cater to individual learning styles rather than a one-size-fits-all educational model. This proactive approach can help prevent the development of self-esteem issues and allow children to develop their strengths and interests without feeling that they are deficient or inadequate.

Neurodivergent individuals, including those with ADHD, autism, dyslexia, auditory and visual processing disorders, and other conditions often have unique cognitive profiles that may not align with conventional educational expectations. These differences are not deficits but variations in thinking and learning. By understanding and supporting neurodivergent traits, educators and parents can help children thrive in their own ways. For example, providing visual aids for a child with dyslexia or allowing more movement breaks for a child with ADHD can make learning more accessible and enjoyable. It's crucial to communicate that these accommodations are not about lowering standards but meeting diverse needs.

Children may also pursue interests and talents outside traditionally valued academic paths, such as art, music, or unconventional hobbies. We should not undervalue these interests or equate success solely with academic achievements. Celebrating and nurturing a child's unique strengths can foster a sense of pride and motivation. This holistic view of success broadens the definition of intelligence beyond conventional academic measures, recognizing the value of creativity, practical skills, and emotional intelligence. Encouraging children to explore their passions, even nontraditional ones, not only enriches their lives but also contributes to a more diverse and innovative society.

Early intervention is key to supporting children with learning differences or unconventional interests. This involves comprehensive assessments (e.g., neuropsychological, occupational therapy) to understand each child's specific needs and strengths, followed by personalized education plans that include appropriate accommodations and support services. It's important that educators, parents, and specialists combine their efforts and experience to meet the child's unique needs. Additionally, fostering an open and ever-evolving dialogue with children about their learning processes helps them understand and embrace their unique ways of learning rather than feeling stigmatized or alienated.

Reinforcing the mindset of fixed intelligence can be damaging to children with learning issues, leading to insecurities about capability, self-doubt, and a fear of failure. Instead, use the growth mindset methodology to emphasize your child's effort and ability to learn, improve, and face challenges. This can empower them to persevere when they are confronted with having to address learning challenges and develop resilience. For example, instead of saying, "You're so smart," you can say, "I'm impressed by how hard you worked on this, how seriously you took this process, and how much you have grown." Spotlight the individual progress and the value of persistence. By doing so, you can help children understand that intelligence and abilities are not static but can grow and develop over time, regardless of any learning challenges they may face.

Success and intelligence are often narrowly defined by societal norms, but it's crucial to adopt a more inclusive and open-minded approach, especially when considering the diverse identities of children. Neurodivergence can challenge standard notions of intelligence and success. Children who may not fit the typical academic mold possess unique strengths and capabilities. Recognizing and valuing these differences is essential. Parents and educators must shift their perspectives to appreciate diverse ways of thinking and learning, emphasizing that intelligence is multifaceted as opposed to limited to traditional academic achievement. Parents and educators should communicate openly with peers, teachers, and community members about the importance of a growth mindset and the value of diverse ways to approach learning.

KEY TAKEAWAYS

- **Importance of Self-Worth and Self-Esteem:** Developing a child's sense of self-worth and self-esteem is essential for their overall identity and mental health. Aim to nurture these qualities consistently.
- **Role of Parenting in Identity Development:** Parenting styles significantly influence a child's identity development. Authoritative parenting, which balances demands with responsiveness, is most effective in fostering a positive self-concept and autonomy.
- **Impact of Impostor Syndrome:** Impostor syndrome is often rooted in childhood experiences where a child's sense of self is heavily reliant on external validation. Preventing this syndrome involves fostering a stable and internalized sense of self-worth.
- **Differentiation between Self-Esteem and Self-Worth:** Self-esteem fluctuates based on achievements and external feedback, whereas self-worth is a constant sense of one's value as a human being. Both need to be nurtured but understood differently.
- **Influence of Secure Attachment:** Secure attachment in early years, characterized by consistent and nurturing care, fosters a positive self-concept and reduces the risk of developing impostor syndrome.

- **Active Listening and Open Dialogue:** Engage in active listening and maintain open dialogue with your child to help them feel valued and understood, which is crucial for their identity development.
- **Role Modeling:** You are a role model; demonstrate healthy behaviors, resilience, and ethical values to help your child internalize these traits and develop a positive sense of self.
- **Identifying Learning Issues and Addressing Neurodivergent Needs:** It is critical to identify learning issues for your child as early as possible, and it is also important to appreciate the unique strengths of neurodivergent children while properly addressing their needs, so they can thrive in a variety of environments.

Chapter Two

FAMILY DYNAMICS AND FORMING HEALTHY RELATIONSHIPS

The next step in the stage of Belonging is helping your child learn to form healthy relationships and feel a sense of belonging and connection in them. With impostor syndrome, it is often common to feel on the fringes, like you do not belong and are often less than those around you. This often results from early childhood experiences when you have felt like you cannot be your full self and like parts of you have had to remain unseen. These fragmented parts often feel unwanted, flawed, or unacceptable and can be part of the experience that you are fraudulent and not as people around you see you.

This chapter explores how to model healthy relational engagement, emphasizes the importance of valuing oneself, teaches how to identify unhealthy and toxic relationships, and offers a guide to end those relationships. As a parent, your role in shaping your child's ability to form healthy relationships (as a child and adult) may arguably be the most important. It starts from their earliest interactions on the playground or in daycare. While teachers and schools will influence their relational development, your impact is crucial in shaping how your child approaches relationships and navigates social dynamics. Additionally, we will examine the family dynamics, roles, and behaviors that should be avoided to prevent the development of impostor syndrome. Understanding how early experiences—whether at home, in school, or in relationships with friends and romantic partners—can shape feelings of insecurity, discomfort, and a lack of autonomy is essential for fostering a healthy sense of power and control in your child.

FAMILY DYNAMICS

As your child grows, their family dynamics play a significant part in how they will view themselves and how they will engage with others. Often, caregivers can be overworked, undervalued, and generally exhausted. Those vulnerable states can get in the way of responding in a more conscious and present way, and instead, we respond in ways that are working (or sometimes not working) to elicit the behavior that we want from the child. For example, we may use language or behavior that is embarrassing, humiliating, or demeaning to get compliance from the child. As humans, we all have our moments, and no one is expecting perfection, but if you engage in these unhealthy behaviors with enough regularity, you will teach your child that they can expect it from other authority or relational figures (teachers, coaches, friends, and eventually, partners), and the outcome that you expect is the outcome that others will expect. As they grow into adults, these children present a greater likelihood to repeat these behaviors and become drawn to authority figures, leaders, and sometimes, even partners who relate to them in the toxic ways in which they grew up. That's because these methods are familiar, tied to connection and love in their minds. We often talk about this early conditioning as *grooving* certain expectations, dynamics, and roles into a child's experience.

AUTHORITY DYNAMICS

Children should understand their personal power and exercise it where appropriate. In certain situations, a child may not be ready for or capable of using their power to determine the best, safest, or most appropriate course of action. This is where your authority as a parent takes precedence. A family's power dynamic should not be upside down, where children are in charge and make determinations about the course and behavior of the family and parents either ignore or follow the direction from the children. It's important to be okay with your parental authority, neither abusing it to maintain control nor using control as a method to cover up other skills that may be lacking (e.g., conflict management, communication, consistent behavior management). Parenting styles play a crucial role in shaping children's self-esteem and their sense of authenticity. Recall our discussion on the three parenting styles, Chapter One.

An adult with impostor syndrome is usually quite deferential in authority situations and has difficulty feeling authorized themselves or internalizing their accomplishments as a method of understanding why they might have authority in a particular situation. In interpersonal dynamics, including those other than work, people with impostor syndrome can find themselves overvaluing the opinions of others and undervaluing those of their own (largely because unless they are negative, they don't believe them). They harbor an intense need to please others and often lack clarity about their future.

The first place where your child will be able to exercise that personal power appropriately is at home. That may be the first place where they can say "no," and someone respects that "no." And that may mean not wanting to do something that their parents want them to do. As in all situations, it's a balance of assessing which things they can exert that personal power with, that is helping them build a healthy sense of autonomy and an independent sense of self, and which decisions may not benefit them in the moment or long-term. In the dynamics of your family, you want to make sure that you are clear about authority as a parent or caregiver, but that children comprehend where their freedom exists to make their own decisions (e.g., in their extracurricular activities, food choices, how they approach studying). Assessing where your children are allowed to make their own choices can be helpful to make sure you understand the areas in which they currently can. Their ability to make their own decisions in a greater number of areas should expand over time when they show greater judgment and skill in using their power in adaptive ways. With authority and power comes responsibility, and this becomes an important piece of teaching your child the balance of personal power. So, with additional authority, there needs to be corresponding responsibility. Responsibility for their actions, but also responsibility for their things, their homes, and those around them. It's also important to be able to assess the new responsibilities that your child may be able to take on developmentally. Each child is unique and, therefore, will be ready for different responsibilities at different times.

CONFLICT MANAGEMENT

People with impostor syndrome can be very conflict-avoidant because of their people-pleasing tendencies. Engaging in conflict in a healthy manner is crucial for personal development and long-term well-being. Conflict is an inevitable part of life, and learning to navigate it effectively helps children develop a healthy sense of self, autonomy, and resilience. By understanding and managing their emotions, communicating clearly, and resolving disputes constructively, children build essential life skills that foster self-confidence and a sense of agency. These skills not only help them in personal interactions but also prepare them for professional and social challenges in adulthood. We will address this in greater detail in Chapter Three.

BEST PRACTICES FOR CONFLICT RESOLUTION

Open communication and emotional expression are paramount to dealing with conflict. Children should be taught to articulate their feelings and thoughts clearly and respectfully, but first, they must have a safe and supportive home environment where they feel comfortable sharing their perspectives without fear of judgment or punishment. Parents and educators can model effective communication by actively listening to children, validating their emotions, and guiding them to express their needs and concerns appropriately. This practice helps children understand that their feelings are important, fostering a positive self-image and self-worth.

Another key aspect of conflict resolution is teaching children problem-solving and negotiation skills. This involves helping them identify the root cause of conflicts and explore possible solutions that consider everyone's needs and perspectives. Facilitate this learning by guiding children through a structured approach to conflict resolution that includes these steps:

- Defining the problem
- Brainstorming potential solutions
- Evaluating the options
- Deciding on the best course of action

These steps approach conflicts thoughtfully and creatively, rather than impulsively, or worse, avoiding the situation altogether.

Setting healthy boundaries and being assertive is essential for preventing people-pleasing behaviors. Children should understand that it is okay to say no. They have the right to protect their personal space and feelings. Educate them on the difference between assertiveness and aggression, emphasizing that being assertive means standing up for oneself respectfully and clearly. Role-playing scenarios and positive reinforcement when children assert their needs appropriately can reinforce these skills. Developing assertiveness helps children maintain their integrity and self-respect, even in challenging situations.

Children often learn behaviors by observing adults, so demonstrate healthy ways to handle disagreements, such as staying calm, listening actively, and seeking compromise. Consistently reinforce these behaviors through praise and encouragement so that your child uses them to help solidify these skills. Additionally, discuss and reflect on past conflicts and their resolutions to provide valuable learning experiences. By consistently modeling and supporting constructive conflict resolution, you help your child internalize these skills, promoting their development into a confident, self-assured individual capable of managing conflict in interpersonal relationships effectively.

RIGID ROLES

When raising children, it can be common to find yourself labeling them in ways that seem to categorize who they are—the "athletic one," "the friendly one," or "the observant one," for instance. Those with impostor syndrome were often characterized as the "smart one" or the "hardworking one." Now it doesn't matter whether they are being called this explicitly or it's implicit in how others behave and talk about them. It's important to see your child in florid detail, not locked in narrow boxes. Rigid roles will limit their understanding of their vast potential. You want to be able to see a multitude of strengths and help them develop where needed.

Howard Gardner's Theory of Multiple Intelligences[6] proposes that individuals possess different kinds of intelligences, each

6 Howard Gardner, *Frames of Mind: The Theory of Multiple Intelligences*, New York: Basic Books, 1983.

reflecting different ways of interacting with the world. Gardner's theory emphasizes that intelligence is not a single, unified attribute that one either possesses or does not possess. Instead, multiple intelligences in varying degrees can be developed and nurtured through appropriate educational experiences and environments. While this model extends our view of what is considered intelligent, it is only meant as a starting point.

Here's a table summarizing Gardner's multiple intelligences:

INTELLIGENCE	DESCRIPTION	EXAMPLES OF SKILLS AND ACTIVITIES
Linguistic	Ability to use language effectively for communication and expression.	Reading, writing, storytelling, learning languages
Logical-Mathematical	Capacity to analyze problems logically, carry out mathematical operations, and investigate issues scientifically.	Problem-solving, conducting experiments, mathematical reasoning
Spatial	Ability to perceive and manipulate visual and spatial elements.	Drawing, designing, navigating, visualizing concepts
Bodily-Kinesthetic	Using one's physical body skillfully and handling objects adroitly.	Dancing, sports, handcrafts, acting
Musical	Skill in performing, composing, and appreciating musical patterns.	Playing instruments, singing, composing music, recognizing rhythms
Interpersonal	Capacity to understand and interact effectively with others.	Communication, empathy, collaboration, conflict resolution

INTELLIGENCE	DESCRIPTION	EXAMPLES OF SKILLS AND ACTIVITIES
Intrapersonal	Insight into one's own emotions, motivations, and inner states.	Self-reflection, self-awareness, emotional regulation
Naturalistic	Interest and skills involving the natural world–plants, animals, and the environment.	Interest in classifying and understanding animals, plants, and aspects of the earth. Connection and comfort with beings and things in nature.
Existential	Awareness and ability to ask and face deep questions about human existence, such as the meaning of life, death, and major life transitions.	Philosophical thinking, pondering life's big questions, spiritual contemplation

People with impostor syndrome tend to view intelligence in very narrow ways, placing themselves within those confines. From their perspective, you either have it or you don't; intelligence feels elusive, idealized, and perfect. For example, they might believe everything comes naturally to someone who is truly intelligent, and that they learn with ease. Now, it's very difficult for everything to come easy all the time, so inevitably, when these individuals struggle, they see it as proof that they are not as intelligent as everyone thinks they are. As a caregiver, it's important to maintain an expansive views of talent and skills. Aim to help your child understand all the beautiful qualities about themselves and foster the yearning in them to grow and develop.

UNDERSTANDING CODEPENDENCE IN PARENTING

Codependent parents overly rely on their children for emotional fulfillment, approval, a sense of purpose, and sometimes even co-parenting of other children. This can lead to unhealthy boundaries and an imbalance in the parent-child relationship. Codependent family relationships can appear as if the family is quite cohesive, but in essence, they cannot operate without each other independently, there is no tolerance for disagreement, and there is a high need for children to be pleasing and agreeable. Avoiding codependence involves fostering independence in children while maintaining a supportive and nurturing environment.

Codependence can lead to impostor syndrome in children. Parents overly involved in their children's lives undermine their children's confidence in their abilities. They may start to feel that their achievements are not truly their own, but rather the result of your involvement. This can contribute to a persistent fear of being exposed as a "fraud" or not being worthy of their success, hallmarks of impostor syndrome. Children raised in codependent relationships may struggle with self-doubt and a lack of internal validation, relying excessively on external approval to gauge their self-worth.

To prevent codependence, it's crucial to set healthy boundaries. This means recognizing and respecting your own emotional needs separately from that of your children. It also involves allowing your children to experience failures and successes on their own, providing guidance rather than control. Strive to be a supportive mentor rather than an authoritarian figure, offering advice when needed but allowing your children to make their own choices. This approach helps them build resilience and learn to trust their judgment, laying the foundation for a healthy, independent adult life.

Open and honest communication is vital in avoiding codependence. Encourage your children to express their thoughts and feelings openly and listen actively without judgment. This creates a safe space for children to explore their identities and build self-esteem. By validating your children's emotions and experiences, you help them develop a strong sense of self-worth. Honest communication also involves an ability to express your needs and feelings appropriately, modeling healthy emotional expression, regulation, and the realization that you are also human with feelings and needs.

IDENTIFYING NARCISSISM IN PARENTING

Narcissistic parents prioritize their own needs, desires, and self-image over their child's well-being. Narcissistic parents often require excessive admiration and validation, lack empathy, and may manipulate their children to serve their own emotional needs. They might also impose unrealistic expectations, criticize excessively, or belittle their children to maintain a sense of superiority. Recognizing these behaviors is crucial for understanding the impact they can have on children, including the potential development of emotional and psychological issues.

Children exposed to narcissistic parenting may develop impostor syndrome stemming from a lack of unconditional support and validation in childhood, where achievements were either overly criticized or not genuinely acknowledged unless they served the parent's self-esteem. As a result, these children grow up internalizing the belief that they are only valued for their achievements, leading to persistent self-doubt and a fear that they are not truly capable or deserving of success.

Avoiding exposure to narcissistic behaviors in parenting involves creating an environment that is conscious of, and prioritizes the child's emotional and psychological needs. Practice self-awareness and reflect on your motivations, behaviors, and history to ensure that you are acting in the best interests of your children. It's also important to seek professional help if you struggle with narcissistic traits, as addressing these issues can significantly improve the family dynamic and the child's emotional health. It is common in our culture to believe that narcissism results from having a high opinion of oneself, but it is often quite the opposite. People who develop narcissistic traits have often been emotionally neglected and have had to create a super-sized version of themselves to believe that they should and could be loved. Their inability to receive criticism is related to their sense of being fragile, and, as one supervisor once told me, a "house of cards" that they are very protective of because if it falls, there is nothing. This can often result in parenting that involves seeking compliance or adoration from children. Children can become what is often referred to as a "narcissistic extension," a piece of the parent and not fully separate from the parent, which is why their child's accomplishments can mean so much to them.

People-pleasing behavior is another common consequence of growing up with a narcissistic parent. Children in such environments often learn to prioritize others' needs and desires over their own as a means of gaining approval or avoiding conflict. Traced back to a childhood where their own needs were frequently overshadowed by those of their parents, this behavior can become deeply ingrained, leading them to constantly seek validation and acceptance from others throughout their lives, to an unhealthy extent. People pleasers often struggle with setting boundaries.

Being raised in a narcissistic household can also predispose individuals to attract and be drawn to narcissistic people in their adult lives. This is often because they have been conditioned to accept and normalize such behavioral patterns, seeing them as familiar and, subconsciously, even comforting. They may also lack a clear understanding of healthy relationship dynamics, making them vulnerable to manipulation and abuse. To break this cycle, it's essential for parents to seek therapy or support groups to develop self-awareness, learn healthy boundary-setting, and rebuild a healthy sense of self. Understanding and acknowledging the impact of your own upbringing can be a critical step toward healing, fostering healthier relationships, and reducing the chance that the cycle will reoccur again.

MODELING HEALTHY RELATIONAL ENGAGEMENT

One of the most important ways that you can support your child's relational style is by modeling healthy relational engagement. Your child is constantly observing, and even if you do not believe they are listening, they are able to take in a lot more information than you may realize. Here are some ways for you to model healthy relational engagement for your child:

- **Emphasize clear and honest communication:** One of the first steps to healthy relational engagement is clear communication. If you have a disagreement, it is vital that you are unambiguous in discussing what the primary issue may be. Further, it is also critical that you are honest in your communication. Your child can tell if you are not being truthful, which can lead them to question their own reality.
- **Limit unhealthy relational engagement:** Engaging in unhealthy behavior, such as yelling, giving someone the silent treatment, stonewalling (i.e., refusing to talk to them because you are angry at them), name-calling, or storming out when you are upset sends a message to your child that these are acceptable forms of behavior. Limiting or eliminating such behavior will illustrate healthier ways to engage relationally.
- **Be transparent about conflict and resolve it intentionally:** Some parents never want their children to see them argue or have a conflict. As we will discuss further in the next chapter, conflict does not have to be bad, and how you manage it is critical to teaching your child healthy relational approaches.

So, if and when you have a conflict, as much as possible, be transparent about the conflict, including what happened and how you resolved it. If you pretend everything is fine, you risk your child feeling that you are gaslighting them. That is, they may not trust their own experience and judgment. Resolution is important because it shows how you utilize your problem-solving, interpersonal, and communication skills to deal with a challenging issue and models good conflict-resolution skills.

- **Apologize sincerely and publicly:** You may feel that apologizing somehow demonstrates weakness, and as a result, you may be reluctant to do so in your relationships. In reality, apologizing shows strength in being able to admit your mistakes or wrongdoing. If you did, in fact, do something that warrants an apology, it is critical that you do so, especially in a sincere manner. A sincere apology sounds like "I am sorry that I offended you," rather than one which is insincere, such as "I am sorry you were offended." The first statement takes responsibility for causing harm to the offended person, while the second one seems to place responsibility on the aggrieved party. Doing this publicly shows your child how conflict is managed in a healthy manner.

VALUING YOURSELF

Another key element to helping your child develop healthy relationships is valuing yourself. This means not allowing others to diminish you, avoiding codependent or toxic relationships, and honoring your worth through your actions. When we devalue ourselves, we let others take advantage of us, do not set appropriate boundaries, and tolerate abusive or toxic behavior. Here are the critical ways you can demonstrate how to value yourself to your child:

- **Not letting others diminish you:** When you stand up for yourself in friendships or romantic relationships, your child learns a valuable lesson. For example, if a partner attempts to berate or belittle you, your child can observe your willingness to defend yourself and voice your belief that such behavior is unacceptable.
- **Setting and maintaining appropriate boundaries:** While some believe that boundaries create undue emotional distance in relationships, the reality is that boundaries signal your ability to manage relationships in a healthy manner. If you have a friend or family member who is constantly violating your boundaries, discuss with them your concerns. For instance, if your mother constantly shows up at your home, even though you have asked her to provide notice before coming, talk to her about honoring boundaries.
- **Not tolerating abusive behavior:** Valuing yourself means not tolerating abusive or toxic behavior, whether physical or emotional. Abusive behavior is physical violence, constant name-calling (e.g., "stupid"), screaming, or emotional manipulation (e.g., making you feel guilty or being a bad partner for not responding right away to their phone call). In these instances, it is important that you model standing up for yourself, not responding similarly and holding the other person accountable, or if you don't feel like you can, seeking the proper support from a therapist about how to handle the situation.

IDENTIFYING UNHEALTHY AND TOXIC RELATIONSHIPS

To help your child know how to form healthy relationships, especially as they grow into preadolescence and adolescence, you must teach them how to identify unhealthy or toxic relationships. Doing so will enable them to recognize the essential signs needed to end such relationships. With impostor syndrome, ending unhealthy relationships is often very difficult. A person is more likely to take too much responsibility in the relationship, feeling embarrassed or guilty about their own flaws and shortcomings that they can't leave or end the relationship.

LISA MOVES ON

In our TEDx talk, "The Impostor Syndrome Paradox: Unleashing the Power of You," Lisa described being stuck in a terrible job with a toxic boss who lied to her, regularly criticized her, and attempted to control her. She spent months feeling trapped in that dysfunctional experience because she felt that she couldn't get another job and no one else would want her. She had the skills to identify unhealthy relationships but didn't have strong skills in exiting relationships that were problematic and struggled to believe that there were better opportunities for her. It took her realizing that her boss was blatantly humiliating her and her colleagues to quit the job and start her own work on her imposter syndrome.

Whether it is with a friend, a romantic partner, or a work colleague (e.g., boss or coworker), here are some relational experiences to teach your child to be mindful of in order to help them identify unhealthy or toxic relationship dynamics:

- **Constant insults or criticism:** Receiving feedback is normal in the development of any relationship and should not be viewed as a negative sign. However, if a friend or partner constantly insults your child by calling them names or criticizing them (e.g., commenting negatively on appearance, interests, or personality), it is evident that the relationship is unhealthy.
- **Love bombing:** In contrast to being insulted constantly, love bombing is when someone emphatically and continually tells your child how wonderful they are without knowing them very well or relentlessly texts or calls them to the point of being overwhelming, especially very early in the relationship. It is often a relational strategy to make your child feel closer to them quickly and intensely without evaluating or getting to know him/her over time. While some may believe that love bombing is simply the way the person shows care, it is usually an indicator of unhealthy relational dynamics and the hiding of other toxic behaviors.
- **Emotional manipulation:** Emotional manipulation is using feelings to get people to do what you want. For instance, if someone tries to make your child feel guilty in order to force them to behave in a certain way or they withhold connection (e.g., freezes your child out when they do something the person doesn't like or cancels plans if they don't immediately respond to a text), that is emotional manipulation. If they threaten to harm themselves if the person does not come to their aid or do what they want, or they attempt to control your

child by telling them what they should do, these are all signs of emotional manipulation.

- **Codependence:** Always being told a person cannot function without you or that they need you to live, leaving you feeling like you cannot have your own needs or set boundaries.
- **Physical or emotional violence:** Physical harm or constant berating (e.g., being told that you are worthless).
- **Endless conflict:** Incessant arguing, with no resolution ever being reached. Unfortunately, some people believe such persistent conflict is a sign of passion or true love. In reality, it is confirmation that the relationship is not healthy and should end.
- **Isolation from loved ones:** If a friend or partner does not want your child to engage with their loved ones, such as family members or other friends, and prevents them from doing so or constantly tracks their whereabouts, an unhealthy relationship dynamic has formed.
- **Persistent violation of boundaries:** As mentioned earlier, boundaries can be protective for your child's well-being and should be honored and respected by those around them. If an individual persistently violates those boundaries (e.g., calls them at all hours of the night, even though they have asked them not to do so after 10 p.m.), that is a red flag.
- **An "on again, off again" cycle:** A never-ending cycle, where they are breaking up, reuniting, breaking up, and reuniting.
- **The need to prove your worthiness or constantly please:** Feeling that your child must prove that they are worthy to be in a relationship, being told how lucky they are to be with

someone, or feeling that their main job in the relationship is to please their friend.

While this list is not exhaustive, these examples are major signs to teach your child to assist them in identifying unhealthy relationships. Once your child is able to do so, they must also know when and how to end such relationships.

WHEN TO END AN UNHEALTHY RELATIONSHIP

With impostor syndrome, initiating the end of a relationship with a difficult or toxic person is very uncomfortable. A person with impostor syndrome may have trouble trusting in themselves and feeling like healthier relationships are out there for them (e.g., they are often more comfortable with the devil they know). They often have trouble utilizing their personal power and authority in relationships, and can stay loyal to another person more than they are loyal to themselves.

Teaching your child skills to end an unhealthy relationship is a key and often very overlooked set of skills. Your child may be fearful or unsure about ending an unhealthy relationship for a variety of reasons. They may feel so emotionally attached to a person that they may be afraid of being alone or losing that connection. They may be concerned about the welfare of the other person. Your child may feel that they are being an unfair or impatient friend or romantic partner who is not giving the relationship ample time to improve. As a parent, you can provide clear and comforting guidance to your child about when and how to end an unhealthy relationship.

You'll want to educate your child about the signs from early on. Provide an opportunity for them to discuss and explore concerns about their relationships. Teach them skills to communicate their needs and boundaries. Teach your child to have zero tolerance for any form of abuse, whether physical or emotional. While your child may be tempted to give their friend or partner a second chance, statistics indicate that someone who is physically or emotionally violent will repeat their behavior, within a brief period of time. For instance, data from a study by Hendricks and his colleagues[7] suggests that 20 percent to 33 percent of domestic violence offenders repeat the infraction within six months. Therefore, such abuse is a major indicator that it is time to end the relationship.

If your child feels their boundaries are constantly violated or they are too often insulted or criticized, it's time to have a conversation about the relationship and point out the issues of concern. Sometimes, a child may not be aware of their unhealthy relational habits, and depending on the nature and depth of the relationship (e.g., the level of intimacy and length of the relationship), it may be useful to bring it to their attention. It is very common for children to be defensive of their friends. Stay regulated in these conversations. It's important to use "I statements" and say things like "I feel sad when I see Kayla yell at you." Focus on the relationship with your child and know that you can revisit it if it gets difficult. You don't have to resolve it in

7 B. Hendricks et al., "Recidivism among Spousal Abusers: Predictions and Program Evaluation," *Journal of Interpersonal Violence* 21, no. 6 (2006): 703–716.

one conversation. Once you bring it to their awareness, then the expectation is that the behavior will change over a reasonable period.

When they are young, elementary school age, you will likely have to intervene and put limits on the relationship (e.g., find other kids to have playdates with/decrease their access to your child, talk to the parents). However, as they get to preadolescence and adolescence, you want to encourage them to have a discussion about undesirable behaviors and their need for a change to occur. If the behavior does not change after such a period, it is time for your child to end the relationship. The skills of holding others accountable and ending unhealthy relationships are critical skills to cultivate in your child because with imposter syndrome, there is often an avoidance of relational conflict and staying in relationships too long. Signs to help your child become aware that it may be time to end an unhealthy relationship are:

- **Refusal to Change Behavior:** When the behavior has been raised and the friend is taking no initiative to change, this could illustrate that likely it's going to stay the same. Behavior change takes time, but you should be able to see the changes even if it is slow and incremental.
- **Lack of Accountability:** If your child's concerns are dismissed or they are gaslighted, told that it is "all in your head," this is a clear indicator that you should terminate the relationship because it is an acknowledgment that they cannot see the concerns and are taking no responsibility and may even seek to place the blame on your child (e.g., the friend tells them that they are just too sensitive when they express their discomfort with constantly being insulted).

- **Persistent Unhappiness:** If you find that your child is consistently unhappy in the relationship and has been for an extended period, despite efforts to address the issues, it may be time to reevaluate the relationship. Relationships should bring joy and fulfillment, not prolonged distress.
- **Loss of Trust:** Trust is the foundation of a healthy relationship. If trust has been broken and cannot be repaired, or if there is a constant feeling of betrayal, suspicion, or dishonesty, it might be a sign that the relationship is no longer viable.
- **Incompatible Values or Goals:** Fundamentally different values, life goals, or visions for the future, with neither party willing or able to compromise, can lead to ongoing conflict and dissatisfaction.
- **Lack of Growth or Stagnation:** If the relationship feels stagnant, with neither person willing or able to grow or evolve, it may indicate that the relationship has run its course. Relationships should foster personal and mutual growth.
- **Unresolved Conflicts and Resentment:** If conflicts and disagreements are frequent and never get resolved, leading to ongoing resentment and emotional distance, it could be a sign that the relationship is no longer working. Continuous unresolved conflict can erode the bond between people.
- **Loss of Respect:** If mutual respect no longer exists and cannot be restored, it's a strong indication that the relationship may need to end.

SKILLS TO END AN UNHEALTHY RELATIONSHIP

Knowing how as well as when to end an unhealthy relationship is essential. Your child may have someone in their life who makes it difficult for them to end the relationship. This person may profusely apologize and promise to change, but never does so. Or they could be ignoring your child's intention to end the relationship and instead increase contact. Therefore, you want to support your child by educating them on the best way to end the relationship. As discussed earlier, if they are in an abusive and dangerous situation, they should leave immediately with the proper protection and support in place. If their safety is not at risk, then here are some strategies to explore.

- **Acknowledge the Toxicity:** The first step in ending a toxic relationship is recognizing and accepting that the relationship is harmful. Be honest with your child about the potential negative impact the relationship has on their mental, emotional, or physical well-being.
- **Plan Your Exit:** Before ending the relationship, plan. They should know what they will do. They should consider the safest and most effective way to communicate the decision, whether that's through a direct conversation, a written message, or with the support of a parent. Having a plan will help them feel more confident and in control.
- **Set Firm Boundaries:** When ending a toxic relationship, set clear and firm boundaries. Your child should communicate what level of contact they want, if any at all, and are

comfortable with moving forward. They should stick to these boundaries to protect themselves from further harm.

- **Seek Support:** Ending a toxic relationship can be emotionally exhausting and traumatizing. Actively seek support from friends, family, or a therapist, as a strong support system can help you stay committed to your decision and provide comfort during the process.
- **Prioritize Self-Care:** After ending a toxic relationship, focus on your recovery, healing and rebuilding your well-being. Engage in activities that bring you joy and relaxation. Give yourself time to learn from the experience and space to repair and recover from the emotional strain of the relationship. Self-care is essential for moving forward in a healthy and positive way.

ELEMENTS OF A HEALTHY RELATIONSHIP

It is also vital to educate your child about the elements of a healthy relationship. Here are some key elements to discuss:

- **They take time to develop.** Healthy, enduring relationships do not happen overnight. Rather, it takes time for both parties to learn about each other. In contrast to unhealthy relationships, where one person attempts to force intimacy too quickly, individuals in a healthy relationship patiently let it develop and do not try to rush the process.
- **Clear, honest communication is a foundational part of a relationship.** Healthy relationships are built on clear, honest

communication, which is most often done in a thoughtful and kind manner.

- **Respect is central to the relationship.** Respect is a core part of the relationship, and each member of the relationship demonstrates it in the way they treat each other.
- **It is collaborative.** Both individuals in the relationship show up in a collaborative way, putting in as much effort as the other to ensure that the relationship remains healthy and each party's needs are being met.
- **Conflict is not avoided and is handled in a mutually beneficial way.** Healthy relationships involve conflict. When there is no conflict in a relationship, it may be a signal that one person in the relationship is unable or afraid to express disagreement. This often leads to a stagnation of growth in one person or both. On the other hand, a healthy relationship manages conflict in a way that is mutually beneficial to all parties. And each party can apologize in a sincere way.
- **There is recognition that it takes work.** Healthy relationships are not static. They continually evolve, as all parties recognize that they are constantly growing as individuals. As such, so should the relationship.

KEY TAKEAWAYS

- **Importance of Family Dynamics:** Family dynamics significantly influence a child's self-perception and relational engagement, starting from their earliest interactions on the playground or in daycare. As a parent, your role in shaping these dynamics is crucial, as it affects how your child navigates relationships and develops a sense of belonging.

- **Avoiding Toxic Family Behaviors:** To prevent the development of impostor syndrome, avoid unhealthy family dynamics that undermine a child's sense of power, control, and autonomy. This includes refraining from using embarrassing or demeaning language to gain compliance from the child.
- **Authority Dynamics:** It's essential to strike a balance in family power dynamics. Exercise your parental authority without abusing it. Teach your child to understand and exercise their personal power in appropriate situations, fostering a healthy sense of autonomy.
- **Valuing Incremental Growth:** Appreciate and celebrate your child's incremental growth rather than only focusing on major achievements. Recognizing small signs of progress to help your child internalize their efforts and skills, reducing the likelihood of developing impostor syndrome.
- **Teaching Conflict Resolution:** Conflict-resolution skills are vital for your child's personal development and long-term well-being. This includes understanding and managing their emotions, communicating clearly, and resolving disputes constructively.
- **Identifying Unhealthy Relationships:** Teach your child to identify unhealthy or toxic relationships. Signs include constant criticism, emotional manipulation, or a partner's attempts to isolate them from loved ones.

- **Modeling Self-Value:** Model self-value by setting and maintaining appropriate boundaries, not tolerating abusive behavior, and demonstrating how to stand up for yourself in relationships. This modeling helps your child learn to value themselves and avoid toxic relationships.

Chapter Three

CONFLICT AND ADVOCATING FOR SELF

The next part of the Belonging phase is handling conflict and self-advocating. Healthy relationships inevitably have conflict. Rather than avoiding conflict or people-pleasing, you can utilize basic conflict-resolution skills and handle conflict while advocating for your needs. In this chapter, we also explore disagreeing without fear of threatening a relationship.

With impostor syndrome, a deep-seated fear of conflict often results in people-pleasing or avoiding out of fear of destroying the relationship or creating conflict that will have negative consequences for it. As a result, people with impostor syndrome tend to avoid conflict at all costs, which can leave them denying their own needs and voice. We want our children to develop conflict-resolution skills and the ability to advocate for themselves.

CONFLICT AND HEALTHY RELATIONSHIPS

As discussed earlier, it's common to believe that conflict is naturally a bad thing that's best avoided. We dislike the uncomfortable feelings that emerge during a conflict and wish to never experience them again. However, it is important to teach your child that conflict, when handled in a healthy manner, can be a positive factor in a relationship. While you do not want to be in constant conflict with someone, knowing how to manage conflict when it periodically occurs can help a relationship grow and thrive over time. It is mutually satisfying when our needs can be discussed and addressed. Explaining the value of engaging with conflict rather than avoiding it can increase your child's ability to effectively handle it in their relationships.

HOW TO DECREASE CONFLICT AVOIDANCE AND PEOPLE-PLEASING

Many individuals dealing with impostor syndrome please those around them, especially individuals with evaluative power (e.g., parents, supervisors, teachers, coaches), to avoid being negatively evaluated and suffering the consequences (e.g., receiving a failing grade, not being considered a "good kid," or losing positive attention). People-pleasing tendencies may also be linked to early childhood experiences with a narcissistic caregiver whose needs were always primary, or in a codependent household where they were expected to have very few needs and not ruffle feathers. Unfortunately, such people-pleasing behaviors come at the expense of one's overall well-being. When a person is so focused on people-pleasing, they neglect their own needs and goals, which can result in unhealthy outcomes (e.g., overwork, burnout, chronic stress). When discussing conflict with your child, explain the value of navigating conflict without excessive people-pleasing or avoidance. Here are some key strategies to do so:

- **Affirm that conflict is a natural part of interpersonal engagement:** Whether it is with a family member, a friend, or a classmate, conflict is a normal part of interpersonal engagement, especially as individuals get to know each other better. Since people come from many varied backgrounds and experiences, it is only natural that they may approach the world differently, resulting in inevitable conflict, which is not a bad thing. Rather, it is an opportunity to clarify misperceptions and explore the needs of each respective person in the relationship.
- **Acknowledge the discomfort of confronting conflict:** Some of what drives conflict avoidance is the feeling of unease associated with confronting an issue or a person related to a tense situation. Therefore, acknowledge that conflict management is uncomfortable yet necessary to maintain and develop healthy relationships.
- **Assert that conflict avoidance and people-pleasing are not healthy relational tactics:** Excessive people-pleasing behaviors and conflict avoidance are not tactics meant to deepen intimacy in relationships. They are utilized as defensive tactics to meet one person's needs while ignoring or dismissing the needs or concerns of the other. Conflict avoidance forces an individual to avoid disagreements that might be resolved

if fully explored. People-pleasing causes the suppression of your own interests in service of preserving an important relationship. Such practices are not features of a truly healthy relationship.

- **Emphasize that one conflict should not lead to the dissolution of a healthy relationship:** Your child may fear that if they have a disagreement with a friend or a partner, it will cause the end of the relationship. Emphasize that one conflict or disagreement should not lead to the dissolution of a relationship. If it does, it may mean that the relationship was not a healthy and sustainable one.

DEVELOPMENT OF BASIC CONFLICT RESOLUTION SKILLS

Now that the necessity of dealing with conflict has been outlined, your child may wonder how to actually develop good conflict-resolution skills. By helping them navigate this arena, you will equip them to handle different conflict scenarios.

LILY'S CONUNDRUM

Lily is a 12-year-old girl who is an only child and has recently been involved in numerous conflicts with her friends at school. She came home one day very upset about a disagreement she had with a group of her friends. Lily told her parents that she didn't know what to do. Her parents realized that they had never discussed conflict-resolution skills with Lily. They explored the cause of the conflict, discussed possible solutions to address it, and helped her practice her response. Lily was able to have a productive conversation with her friends and resolve the conflict.

Conflict resolution is not an innate talent that everyone possesses. It needs to be taught, and your child will gain from your guidance and skills to manage conflicts in the most effective manner. Before discussing the steps to basic conflict resolution, it is useful to explore the different approaches to handling conflict. Ken W. Thomas and Ralph H. Kilmann created a model that identifies five modes of handling conflict based on how assertive or cooperative an individual is. In their model, assertiveness refers to the extent to which an individual attempts to have his concerns addressed, and cooperativeness refers to the extent to which an individual tries to cater to the concerns of others. The five modes of conflict management in the Thomas-Kilmann model are as follows:[8]

1. **Avoiding:** Low assertiveness, low cooperativeness. In this mode, an individual is not seeking to address a conflict at all and may delay or altogether avoid the issue. This is viewed as a "lose-lose" position.

2. **Accommodating:** Low assertiveness, high cooperativeness. In this mode, an individual seeks to meet the concerns of the other party while failing to voice their own concerns. This is regarded as a "lose, win" position.

---

8 K. W. Thomas and R. H. Kilmann (1976). Thomas-Kilmann Conflict Mode Instrument. Group & Organization Studies, 1, 249-251.

3. Competing: High assertiveness, low cooperativeness. In this conflict-handling mode, an individual is primarily concerned with addressing their needs in a conflict. This is seen as a "win, lose" position.

4. Compromising: Moderate assertiveness and cooperativeness. In this mode, individuals attempt to find an expedient solution that can partially satisfy all parties. This is viewed as a "win-win" position.

5. Collaborating: High assertiveness, high cooperativeness. This conflict-handling approach features individuals who are looking for a solution that can completely satisfy the concerns of all parties. This is considered a "win-win" approach.

All individuals are capable of utilizing all the approaches, but one can rely heavily on one or another based on temperament and the situation at hand. Generally, utilizing a "win-win" approach (e.g., Compromising or Collaborating) would seem to be the optimal option, and Avoiding would be the least useful one. Yet, in some scenarios (e.g., one in which an individual has less power or is seeking favor), it may be helpful to utilize one of the other approaches (e.g., Accommodating).

Explore your child's natural preference and how they may need to adapt their approach, given the situation.

The following steps teach your child about basic conflict-resolution skills:

1. Help your child identify what the conflict is about: Sometimes, when a disagreement occurs, your child may not even be clear about the nature of the conflict. Therefore, the first step in the process of conflict resolution is to identify the actual conflict.

2. Seek to articulate their position: Once they identify the source of the conflict, your child should be able to articulate their position. In this moment, they may be tempted to use an Avoiding or Accommodating approach rather than voice their position for fear of upsetting the other person or disrupting the relationship. As noted earlier, healthy relationships should be able to tolerate conflict and engage with it in a productive manner.

3. Attempt to find common ground rather than a "win-lose" position: Often, when a disagreement occurs, both parties involved may immediately seek to "win" the argument, which makes it difficult to find common ground. By genuinely seeking common ground, your child can learn to recognize shared points of concern (e.g., both parties may be upset about being misunderstood), which can make the conflict easier to defuse.

4. De-escalate when possible: When emotions are high during a conflict, it can easily lead to an escalation, which can have negative outcomes. Therefore, teach your child to de-escalate when possible by keeping a calm demeanor, not raising their voice, and seeking to maintain a respectful dialogue. In situations where they may not feel safe, you should teach them to exit the environment.

5. Minimize acrimony: Personal attacks or name-calling never help to solve a conflict but rather escalate it in ways that are not helpful to any party. Teach your child to stay focused on the issue at hand and use "I" statements to highlight feelings (e.g., "When you said X, it made me feel dismissed and angry.") and minimize acrimony.

6. Find a collaborative or compromising resolution: In the best-case scenario of conflict resolution, both parties can find a resolution that partially or completely satisfies their concerns. The essential aspect of conflict management is actually reaching a resolution. So many conflicts continue over time because the people involved never truly resolve the issue or accept the resolution. For your child, in coming to this resolution, teaching them how to take a collaborative, or compromising approach can enable both parties to feel that their needs are being met, if not fully, at least partially.

WHY CONFLICT IS SO IMPORTANT TO RELATIONSHIPS

Approaching conflict constructively allows individuals to address underlying issues, clear up misunderstandings, and establish clearer communication channels. For someone struggling with impostor syndrome who may already harbor insecurities about their self-worth and authenticity, conflict can provide a necessary opportunity to voice concerns and fears that might otherwise remain unspoken. This process of open communication not only alleviates internal tensions but also fosters a deeper understanding and connection between the individuals involved.

Conflict resolution can lead to greater confidence and assertiveness. Often, individuals with impostor syndrome struggle with people-pleasing tendencies and a reluctance to express their true thoughts or feelings for fear of being judged or rejected. Advocating for oneself and standing firm in one's values and beliefs can lead to a significant boost in self-esteem, as the person learns that their voice matters and they are not defined by others' perceptions. This helps them recognize their own strength and resilience, reinforcing their sense of identity and reducing the grip of impostor syndrome.

Additionally, conflict can be instrumental in reshaping the dynamics of a relationship, making it healthier and more balanced. For individuals with impostor syndrome, relationships can sometimes become skewed, with one person overly accommodating to avoid conflict. Effective conflict management allows both parties to renegotiate boundaries and expectations, ensuring that the relationship is mutually supportive rather than one-sided. This process not only improves the quality of the relationship but also provides the individual with impostor syndrome the reassurance that their needs and feelings are valid and worthy of consideration, helping to dismantle the false beliefs that fuel their insecurities.

HOW YOU CAN MODEL CONFLICT MANAGEMENT

During a disagreement with your child, model healthy conflict-resolution skills in real time. This is a powerful way to teach them. The first step is to stay calm and emotionally regulated, even when their emotions may be intense. Children are highly perceptive and will take cues from your behavior, especially in tense situations. Demonstrate that it is possible to address issues without resorting to shouting or anger. This helps create a safe environment where your child feels heard and understood rather than threatened or defensive. It also shows that conflicts can be resolved through rational discussion rather than emotional outbursts.

Next, use clear and respectful communication. When addressing the conflict, express your feelings and concerns using "I" statements, such as "I feel upset when..." Contrary to what many people believe, it is okay to express with your children how you feel; likely, they know it already from how you are responding, and it lets them know that you are human and have real feelings too. This approach focuses on your own experience rather than placing blame on your child, which can reduce defensiveness and open the door to a more productive conversation. Encourage your child to share their perspective as well and listen actively to what they have to say. Do not contradict them or put your own point of view forward at this point. Fully hear your child out. This two-way dialogue begins a process of resolving the immediate issue while teaching your child the importance of expressing their feelings and listening to others in a respectful manner.

Finally, emphasize the importance of finding a solution together. Rather than dictating the outcome, involve your child in the process of resolving the conflict. Ask questions like, "What do you think we can do to make this better?" or "How can we avoid this problem in the future?" This collaborative approach not only empowers your child by giving them a voice in the resolution but also teaches them that conflicts are opportunities for growth and problem-solving. By working together to find a solution, you reinforce the idea that conflicts can be resolved in a way that meets the needs of everyone involved, fostering a sense of teamwork and mutual respect in your relationship.

KEY TAKEAWAYS

- **Conflict as a Positive Force:** Healthy relationships inevitably involve conflict, and it's important to understand that conflict, when managed constructively, can lead to growth, deeper understanding, and stronger connections. Teaching your children the value of conflict can help them navigate relationships more effectively.
- **Impostor Syndrome and Conflict Avoidance:** Individuals with impostor syndrome often fear conflict, leading to people-pleasing and avoidance behaviors. This fear stems from a concern that conflict might expose their perceived inadequacies or harm their relationships, which can result in them neglecting their own needs.
- **Teaching Conflict-Resolution Skills:** Children need to learn basic conflict-resolution skills to manage disagreements effectively. Parents can play a critical role in this by guiding their children through conflict scenarios, helping them articulate their positions, and finding common ground.
- **Dismantling People-Pleasing Tendencies:** Teach children that excessive people-pleasing and conflict avoidance are unhealthy relational tactics. These behaviors can lead to burnout and stress, and they often prevent the development of authentic, balanced relationships.

- **Modeling Healthy Conflict Management:** Model healthy conflict resolution by staying calm, using respectful communication, and involving your children in finding collaborative solutions. This approach teaches them how to handle conflicts constructively and ensures that their voices are heard.
- **Conflict as an Opportunity for Growth:** Instead of viewing conflict as something to be feared, it's important to teach children that it can be an opportunity for growth, problem-solving, and strengthening relationships. By addressing conflicts openly, children learn to advocate for themselves and develop confidence in their ability to navigate challenging situations.

Chapter Four

PERFORMANCE ANXIETY

One of the more challenging issues that many children face is performance anxiety. The American Psychological Association defines performance anxiety as "apprehension and fear of the consequences of being unable to perform a task or of performing it at a level that will raise expectations of even better task achievement."[9] This chapter will examine how you can help your child manage performance anxiety in productive ways, including replacing negative self-talk with positive self-talk statements, using mindfulness and emotional regulation techniques, and setting healthy expectations. This chapter will also discuss how to assist your child in regulating their affect in a performance situation, such as using breathing techniques, mindfulness, and identifying their range of emotions. We will also cover how to help your child manage performance expectations, including reducing perfectionism and people-pleasing.

9 "Performance Anxiety," APA Dictionary of Psychology, s.v. "performance anxiety," dictionary.apa.org/performance-anxiety, accessed March 12, 2024.

THE IMPOSTOR SYNDROME CYCLE I

THE IMPOSTOR SYNDROME CYCLE II

Performance anxiety is inextricably linked to impostor syndrome. It begins the impostor syndrome cycle, which typically looks like one of two cycles.

Example: Performance anxiety > Overwork or Self-Sabotage > Performance Review > Reject Positive Feedback and/or Hyper-focus on Negative Feedback

JASON'S COMPETITION FEARS

Jason is an 11-year-old fencer who has been competing in local tournaments for about six months. When he first started the sport, he enjoyed the ability to wield a sword and felt very connected to his fencing club. However, when he began to compete, his parents noticed a change in him. The night before his competitions, he would complain of an upset stomach. On the day of his fencing event, Jason would have difficulty waking up and tell his parents that he did not want to compete. His parents would need to convince him to go to the fencing tournament, and the whole ride there, Jason would cry and say he didn't feel well. Jason would participate and do relatively well (but below expectations) despite his reluctance. He would repeat the same cycle for each subsequent tournament. His parents were confused by what they were seeing and frustrated by his lack of success in these tournaments because Jason would do so much better in practice.

UNDERSTANDING PERFORMANCE ANXIETY

Whether it is competing in a sport, giving a presentation in front of a class, taking an important test, or playing an instrument, your child will find themselves in a variety of performance situations. And as a result, they may deal with performance anxiety. Test anxiety is one of the most common forms of performance anxiety for children. Another is competition-related performance anxiety, similar to what Jason was experiencing. When Jason's parents finally asked him about his reluctance to go to his fencing competitions, he told them that he didn't want to lose in front of all those people, that he started to worry that he wouldn't win any of his fencing bouts and he would disappoint them, his coaches, and other people who had expectations of him. Jason's parents attempted to allay his fears about his fencing performance by telling him he would do fine. However, they found that the feedback was not helpful to him, and he kept repeating the same patterns. The key to truly helping Jason was for his parents to use techniques that are research-backed and shown to be effective in addressing the components of his performance anxiety.

It's important to understand that when we are dealing with performance anxiety, the complete elimination of anxiety is not the goal. Research has found that a moderate amount of anxiety is beneficial to performance and actually improves it. Our goal is to ensure enough anxiety for alertness, attention, and enhanced performance, but not so much that it does the opposite.

Now, depending on your relationship with the child experiencing performance anxiety, your role in the process will vary. If you are the coach, the child's technical performance will be in your sphere of influence, but if you are the parent, it should not be (e.g., you are not a baseball coach). As an adult, your job is to understand two primary things: 1) What is your role for your child? 2) What does your child need from you when they are experiencing performance anxiety?

WHAT IS YOUR ROLE?	WHAT DOES YOUR CHILD NEED FROM YOU?
Teacher of the Skill (e.g., teacher, coach, instructor)	Focus on the development of the skill.
Parent, Relative, Caregiver	Focus on the socio-emotional development process.
Supporter	Support the emotional process that their caregivers are working on (if healthy).

May a teacher or coach also need to support a child emotionally? Of course! However, the caregivers need to be the primary persons consistently providing that healthy developmental support, not the teacher or coach. The teacher/coach/instructor should not be the primary emotional support system for the child for a variety of reasons: they may not be consistent, they may have maladaptive ways of providing support, or they have a variety of other children to attend to.

Can the parent or caregiver comment on the child's technique (e.g., the instrument, sport, academic skill)? Probably not. You should leave that in the hands of the competent professionals you have around you to build those particular skills for your child.

If you have true technical skills in that area, you can comment. But remember that whatever you say to your child will likely carry the most weight, so be clear about what you are trying to communicate and why you are trying to communicate this to your child. It should be to help them build a particular skill or technique or develop some awareness, but it shouldn't be because you are ashamed or embarrassed by their performance or have set some expectation that has nothing to do with them and more to do with you and your needs. You can comment on the process that they may be responsible for under your purview, such as their practice schedule, the following up with homework, their ability to take feedback from their instructors, their behavior with teammates and classmates, and their process in general. However, it's best to choose the moments to address these things strategically—the child should be emotionally regulated and more readily able to take in the feedback (i.e., not immediately after a tough loss or a poor performance).

Let's break up the performance anxiety into three phases: before the event, during the event, and after the event. It will be helpful to think about what intervention strategies can be most helpful to address which part of the process. Certain phases can be more anxiety-provoking for your child and others relatively less.

Here are a few experiences that you may see when your child exhibits performance anxiety. It's important to note which incidences are particularly troubling for your child and which ones are hard for you as the caregiver. Awareness of this can help suggest moments where you may be vulnerable and have difficulty providing the support you need for your child.

AUTOMATIC NEGATIVE THOUGHTS

Automatic Negative Thoughts (ANTs) are irrational thoughts that come to mind when you are triggered and typically are negative. Here are some examples.

Mind-Reading: Assuming people are thinking negatively without any evidence. ***Example:*** "Everyone thinks I don't belong in this sport."

Fortune-Telling: Predicting the future negatively. ***Example:*** "I won't be able to beat any of my opponents today."

Catastrophizing: Considering the worst case scenario when imagining outcomes. ***Example:*** "I will not perform well and everyone will laugh at me."

Labeling: Attributing negative character traits to yourself. ***Example:*** "I am very stupid when it comes to social interactions."

Dichotomous Thinking: Engaging in all or nothing thinking. ***Example:*** "If I fail this test today, I will never be able to get into college."

Discounting Positives: Claiming that positive things you do are trivial. ***Example:*** "My coach told me I am making good progress, but he just wants me to feel good and didn't really mean it."

Personalizing: Assigning blame to yourself for negative events, failures, or mistakes and being unable or unwilling to see that some events are caused by others. ***Example:***

"I know that it is my fault that the group project did not go well, even though I did my part. I should have made sure that my other group members were prepared and completed their tasks on time."

Negative Filtering: Focusing only on the negative aspects of a situation and ignoring the positive ones. ***Example:*** "I made one huge mistake on the presentation today, and even though everyone said it went well, I think it was a disaster."

Unfair Comparisons: Comparing apples to oranges—making comparisons to people who are more experienced, are older, and have a different context. ***Example:*** "All these ranked tennis players are so much better than me."

Regret Orientation: Obsessing about what negative things you did in the past; ignoring your agency in the present moment to do something different now. ***Example:*** "I am so angry that I wasn't able to improve my violin playing sooner. I could have been an incredible violinist."

Emotional Reasoning: Interpreting your feelings as what is truly happening to you and not recognizing that your feelings may not let you accurately interpret the moment. ***Example:*** "I felt nervous during my presentation, so everyone can see how anxious I was and the poor job I did."

Inability to Disconfirm: Finding it difficult to disprove your ANTs and actually looking for evidence that they are true and accurate. ***Example:*** "It is a fact that I am not qualified to do this job well, because my boss has never given me any feedback."

BEFORE THE PERFORMANCE:

- Anticipatory Worry: worrying about things before they happen
- ANTs Repertoire: Catastrophizing, Fortune-telling, Labeling, Negative Filtering, Emotional Reasoning, Judgment Focus, What If's, Inability to Disconfirm
- Somatization: e.g., stomach aches, headaches, nausea that do not have a biological basis (illness, injury, etc.)
- Difficulty with practice, warming up, or rehearsal before the event because it increases anxiety

DURING THE PERFORMANCE:

- Extreme anxiety, which impairs performance
- ANTs Repertoire: Catastrophizing, Fortune-telling, Labeling, Emotional Reasoning,
- Dysregulation (e.g., emotional highs and lows, irritability)
- Disorientation and trouble feeling grounded

AFTER THE PERFORMANCE:

- Difficulty regulating back to baseline
- Fear and avoidance of future events
- ANTs Repertoire – Catastrophizing, Negative Filtering, Dichotomous Thinking, Shoulds, Unfair Comparisons, Emotional Reasoning, Personalizing, Regret Orientation, Overgeneralization, Discounting Positives
- Difficulty internalizing positive feedback
- Hyperfocusing on negative experiences, feedback

- Trouble internalizing constructive feedback or managing parental expectations

Once you have noted the particular areas that are difficult for your child and exacerbating their performance, let's then consider how you can intervene. Remember, what's most important about interventions is that you have to use them consistently, over and over again, until your child has internalized them and uses them on their own without guidance or support. You are looking for incremental change over periods of time, and once they have that part of the technique, you can let them take over. But it takes many repetitions, and it's crucial that you appreciate the repetitive nature. Don't fault your child for needing it.

STRATEGIES TO REDUCE PERFORMANCE ANXIETY

BEFORE THE PERFORMANCE

Emotional regulation and positive mental rehearsal are the name of the game when it comes to dealing with performance anxiety issues before an event. Let's begin with emotional regulation first. Emotional regulation is the ability of an individual to modulate an emotion or set of emotions.[10] We will specifically address explicit emotional regulation here, which is the use of conscious monitoring or particular techniques to produce a

10 "Emotional Regulation," APA Dictionary of Psychology, American Psychological Association, dictionary.apa.org/emotion-regulation, accessed March 19, 2024.

more positive outcome. By the age of five, typically, kids have developed to the point when they have emotional regulation skills. At about this age, you may want to incorporate techniques they can regularly utilize to actively engage in emotional regulation. Before this age, we should teach children a robust vocabulary to name emotions, to locate the feelings in their body, appropriate ways to express emotions and behaviors that are maladaptive (e.g., hitting, hurting, denying), and modeling for them with our behavior how to best regulate.

Often, we as adults have not been taught basic emotional regulation techniques and are using methods that we have adopted along the way that may or may not be working. So, perhaps this is the first time you yourself are really considering your process with emotional regulation. It's important that you have these skills before your child or the child you are supporting does. Here are some of the basics that we need to put in place:

MINDFULNESS MEDITATION

The Greater Good Science Center at the University of California Berkeley calls mindfulness meditation the practice of using meditation to maintain "a moment-by-moment awareness of our thoughts, feelings, bodily sensations, and surrounding environment, through a gentle, nurturing lens."[11] Research has shown mindfulness meditation to reduce emotional dysregulation, increase emotional processing, and enhance cognitive

---

11 Greater Good Science Center, "Mindfulness Definition," *Greater Good Magazine*, https://greatergood.berkeley.edu/topic/mindfulness/definition, accessed May 29, 2024.

functioning.[12] The amount of time to engage in mindful meditation for impact does vary, but what comes across from the research is that consistency of practice matters most. To give you a ballpark, try to commit to a practice of about 5 to 40 minutes per day, which can be split over several sessions. While you may see many techniques purported as the best or most impactful, it's really about what you and your child enjoy and will stick to. Remember, you must model the behavior that you want to see.

When you are working on mindfulness meditation practices, do not aim for perfection (i.e., trying to attain complete focus or a lack of interference); aim instead for consistency, creating space for meditation in your everyday life. So, before an event, if your child is practicing mindfulness meditation, they may increase it a little bit that week or do a specific one that they like for tense or high-performance situations.

The following are some ways to practice mindful meditation.

Belly Breathing: Encourage children to lie down comfortably and place their hands on their bellies. Instruct them to take deep breaths in through their noses and feel their bellies rise, then slowly exhale and feel their bellies fall. This exercise helps them focus on their breathing and can be very calming.

How to Practice: "Close your eyes and take a deep breath in through your nose, letting your belly fill up like a balloon. Now,

12 Ruchika Shaurya Prakash, "Mindfulness Meditation: Impact on Attentional Control and Emotion Dysregulation," *Archives of Clinical Neuropsychology* 36, no. 7 (October 2021): 1283–90, https://doi.org/10.1093/arclin/acab053; R. Wu, L. Liu, H. Zhu, W. Su, Z. Cao, S. Zhong, X. Liu, and C. Jiang, "Brief Mindfulness Meditation Improves Emotion Processing," *Frontiers in Neuroscience* 13 (2019): 1074, https://doi.org/10.3389/fnins.2019.01074.

slowly breathe out through your mouth, feeling your belly go back down. Let's do this a few times together."

Five Senses Exercise or 5-4-3-2-1 Technique: Focusing on their senses helps children ground when they are feeling anxious or panicky. Ask them to notice five things they can see, four things they can touch, three things they can hear, two things they can smell, and one thing they can taste.

How to Practice: "Let's play a game called 'Five Senses.' Look around and find five things you can see. Now, close your eyes and find four things you can touch around you. Next, listen carefully and tell me three things you can hear. Take a big sniff and find two things you can smell. Finally, notice one thing you can taste."

Body Scan: Guide children through a body scan, helping them focus on different parts of their bodies, starting from their toes and moving up to their heads. This helps them become aware of physical sensations and promotes relaxation.

How to Practice: "Close your eyes and lie down comfortably. Let's start by wiggling your toes, then noticing how your feet feel. Move up to your legs, then your tummy, your chest, and your arms. Finally, notice how your head and face feel. If you feel any tension, imagine it melting away like ice in the sun."

Gratitude Practice: Encourage children to think about or write down three things they are grateful for each day. This helps shift their focus to positive aspects of their lives and promotes a sense of well-being.

How to Practice: "Let's take a moment to think about three things you're grateful for today. It could be something fun you did, a kind friend, or a yummy meal. If you want, you can draw or write them down to remember them."

Being in the right mindset before an event is critical to deal with performance anxiety. Negative self-talk can really get in the way of positive mental preparation for the event.

COUNTERING NEGATIVE SELF-TALK

One of the reasons that the intervention by Jason's parents did not sufficiently work is that they did not realize the frequency and intensity of the negative self-talk that Jason engaged in, especially before a fencing tournament. The APA Dictionary of Psychology defines negative self-talk as "the internal dialogue which an individual has with herself, which confirms or reinforces negative beliefs and attitudes, such as fears and false aspirations, which have a correspondingly negative effect on the individual's feelings (e.g., a sense of worthlessness) and reactions (e.g., demotivation)."[13] Jason's inner voice would tell him, "You are going to lose," and "You may not even score a touch today." Although they had good intentions, Jason's parents could not counter the barrage of negative self-talk messages Jason would receive from his inner voice. Telling him everything would be fine was too vague of a statement.

The key to countering negative self-talk is consistently replacing it with positive self-talk, reinforcing positive beliefs and attitudes. Since your child may not be familiar with negative and positive self-talk, as a caregiver, it will be important to support them in this practice. According to the APA Dictionary of Psychology,

13 American Psychological Association, "Self-Talk," APA Dictionary of Psychology, accessed May 29, 2024, https://dictionary.apa.org/self-talk.

in sports, positive self-talk also provides cues to the body to act in particular ways, to cue attentional focus, to motivate, to reinforce self-efficacy, and to facilitate the creation of an ideal performance state, which is the state of cognitive and physiological activation that permits optimal performance for an individual.[14]

Here are some examples of how to replace a negative self-talk statement with a positive self-talk statement.

EXAMPLE #1

Negative self-talk statement: "I am going to lose every bout during my fencing tournament."

Positive self-talk statement: "I am going to use the skills and knowledge that I have gained from my fencing lessons and practice to fence my best. I believe I can do well because I have prepared for these moments."

EXAMPLE #2

Negative self-talk statement: "Everyone will laugh at me when I give my speech in school tomorrow. I am going to make a fool out of myself."

Positive self-talk statement: "I have practiced my speech numerous times, I am ready, and I know I will do a good job delivering it."

EXAMPLE #3

Negative self-talk statement: "I am going to fail this test, and it will really bring my grades down."

---

14 Magdalena Kruk et al., "Mental Strategies Predict Performance and Satisfaction with Performance among Soccer Players," *Journal of Human Kinetics* 59 (October 20, 2017): 79–90, doi: 10.1515/hukin-2017-0149.

Positive self-talk statement: "I have studied for weeks for the test, know the content, and am confident that I will do well."

When attempting to counter negative self-talk, in addition to teaching your child how to replace it with positive self-talk, teach your child these other critical elements:

- **Naming it.** The negative self-talk is so familiar and automatic that your child may not even recognize it as such. They may view it as factual information about themselves (e.g., "I am not a good fencer") rather than negative beliefs and attitudes that may have no basis in reality. Therefore, it will be helpful to your child to recognize that the inner voice speaking to them is actually negative self-talk and not true or their own authentic voice. By identifying it, your child can then work to counter it with positive self-talk.
- **Consistency.** When negative self-talk begins to emerge, you must teach your child to replace it with positive self-talk immediately. Oftentimes, the negative self-talk happens so quickly that your child may forget to replace it. However, being consistent with replacing negative self-talk with positive self-talk will make it more likely that the negative self-talk can be extinguished or greatly reduced over time.
- **Persistence and patience.** As a parent, you may become frustrated when you notice that your child's negative self-talk does not magically disappear after you teach them about the concept and how to replace it. Your child may feel that same sense of frustration. Therefore, it is so valuable to realize that your child is now trying to condition their mind to think in a different, more positive way after many years of being conditioned to think in a negative self-talk way. Thus, it will

take persistence and patience on both your parts as your child works on reducing their negative self-talk.

- **Observation of role models.** Sometimes, you may not be aware of how much your child is observing your words and actions. Recognize that if you are teaching your child about counteracting negative self-talk but they hear you engaging in it out loud (e.g., "I am not going to do well on that work presentation tomorrow") without positive self-talk replacement, they may follow your example and continue to engage in negative self-talk. However, if your child frequently observes you using positive self-talk (e.g., "I am excited about the talk I am going to do tomorrow, and I am ready to do a great job"), it will serve as a powerful model for them to do the same.

After consulting with Jason's therapist and realizing that the issue was performance anxiety, his parents were able to teach him about negative self-talk and how to replace it with positive self-talk, which greatly reduced his performance anxiety. Although he feels nervous before a tournament, Jason also feels excited about fencing and looks forward to his tournaments.

POSITIVE MENTAL REHEARSAL

Preparing for an event can be an important part of contending with performance anxiety. Avoidance can be a very familiar part of the anxiety that can cause your child not to practice, discuss, or deal with the event, project, or performance ahead of time. These are often wonderful times to introduce a mindfulness meditation before engaging in the practice session to reduce emotional reactivity.

It can also be very helpful for your child to do an imaginative rehearsal of the day with a positive and desired outcome. In this exercise, your child would close their eyes and either sit back or lie down and visualize the entire event from beginning to end. You want them to see all the details, imagine how their body feels, visualize what the room looks like and sounds like, imagine the behaviors that will engage them and who else will be there, and finally, imagine a positive outcome. Your child should use and imagine all five senses (smell, touch, sound, taste, and sight). They can even do it more than once in preparation for the event.

Imaginative rehearsal can also be used to imagine feared outcomes. The exercise only changes in that your child imagines the things that they fear or worry might happen during the event. But this time, they decide how they will respond to any potential negative happenings in a more positive way for them. If a negative outcome is imagined, your child can also recognize that it comes and goes and that they can tolerate and sit with that uncomfortable and difficult sensation.

For effective mental rehearsal, it's important that your child:

- Be free of distractions (as much as possible)
- Attend to all of their senses
- Prepare for many possible outcomes and variable moments (positive, difficult, and in-between)
- Repeat the technique many times, as it will become more comfortable over time

Mental rehearsal increases readiness, confidence, resilience, and focus in challenging situations. Athletes who've used mental rehearsal before games showed lower levels of anxiety and stress during the event.[15] Teaching your child mental rehearsal helps them to prepare for any performance event (e.g., school testing, musical performances, high-stress social activities) in a way that can make the experience more enjoyable and less stressful. The practice of mental rehearsal can also help a child build their sense of capability and ability to tolerate tough situations and attentional resources in the moment.

DURING THE PERFORMANCE

It's important for your child to recognize that a moderate amount of anxiety is normal. The aim should not be the total absence of anxiety. It is unrealistic and likely unattainable. In reality, a moderate amount of anxiety improves performance by heightening alertness, focus, arousal, and motivation. The key is to keep it in the moderate range (known as the Yerkes-Dodson Law), and this is accomplished through the use of mindfulness meditation, keeping performance routines consistent (the predictability helps to regulate and set expectations about how the event will go), and caring for the mind and body so it maintains optimal performance (e.g., sleep, nutrition, and hydration).

As a parent, keeping things structured, consistent, and predictable when your child has to perform helps to provide a healthy container (i.e., someone that you can trust to hold

---

15 Zahari Jaafa and R. Mohar Kassim, "The Effectiveness of Imagery Training on Anxiety Levels and Performance amongst Athletes in Archery," *Australian Journal of Basic and Applied Sciences* 10, no. 11 (2016): 207–213; S. Mousavi and A.F. Meshkini, "Effect of Mental Imagery upon the Reduction of Athletes Anxiety during Sport Performance," *International Journal of Academic Research in Business and Social Sciences* (2011): 97–108; S. Mousavi and A.F. Meshkini, "Effect of Mental Imagery upon the Reduction of Athletes Anxiety during Sport Performance," *International Journal of Academic Research in Business and Social Sciences* (2011): 97–108.

behaviors that feel safe and regulated) for stressful moments. It's also important as a parent to regulate yourself well when you are around your child. I am sure that you have seen situations with a dysregulated coach or parent that does, in fact, produce a solid result. For example, your child's coach may yell at a player during a match, and that player then begins to perform better. This kind of situation can reinforce the idea that yelling, being tough with, or berating your child can produce positive results. While yes, it may produce results temporarily, that child will either require that kind of berating to perform in the future or internalize it and do it to themselves, which often results in poor self-esteem and self-efficacy beliefs, codependent behavior (requiring external validation or criticism to perform), and unhealthy practices around performance. We are definitely not aiming for that. In addition to a strong performance, we are looking for a healthy and well-adjusted child with long-term positive outcomes (e.g., high self-esteem).

If dysregulated behavior happens during the event, you want to provide a supportive container (i.e., allow for the expression of emotions in healthy ways) but not to provide corrective feedback in the moment. In a dysregulated state, it is very difficult to process corrective feedback, and you want your child to be able to return to a regulated state before the feedback.

AFTER THE PERFORMANCE

The moment after a performance is such an important time. It's a time for celebration. It's a time to process experiences and feelings. It's a time for learning and revisions to the preparation process. Similarly, you want to ensure that your child is regulated when you do any of these things because you want it to have a long-lasting impact.

REGULATION TO BASELINE AFTER THE EVENT

High-stress performance events can be very emotionally dysregulating and can tax your nervous system. Helping your child find their baseline, which is their normal state of functioning, is a critical skill to teach. You should have a down-regulating ritual that keeps your child from being stuck in a heightened, agitated, or intense emotional state. Once you have found that ritual, you want to stick with it as a matter of course. Here are some things you might want to include in that process:

- Verbal processing—discussing the experience of the performance
- Meditation
- Music
- A bath or shower
- Movement/stretching/yoga
- Self-massage

CELEBRATING THE GRAY OF SUCCESS

With impostor syndrome, success can be seen in black-and-white terms: you either won or lost or performed poorly or fantastically. But your job as an adult is to help your child see the nuance and the gray. You want them to pay attention to incremental growth (i.e., the things they are doing even slightly better). You want to celebrate all kinds of success, not just a medal, first place, or trophy. You want to celebrate regulating emotions better, enjoying the experience, a new risk they took, and stepping outside of their comfort zone. You want to focus on growth, especially your child's own individual growth and goals in every shape that might take place. These should get a clear celebration.

You also want to frame mistakes as opportunities for learning. Mistakes are just as valuable as success and doing things "right." It's important for your child to understand that mistakes will likely happen throughout their lifetime of learning, and what's most crucial is what they learn from the mistake and not the mistake itself. Your child should practice embracing mistake-making and recognizing that this is the zone where you stretch yourself, take risks, and allow your humanness to propel you forward. Perfectionism can limit you, prevent you from growing, and keep you stuck in issues of mastery.

SETTING HEALTHY EXPECTATIONS

Another key strategy to reduce your child's performance anxiety is to discuss healthy expectations related to their performance, especially concerning people-pleasing and perfectionism. Many children want to do well to impress and please their parents, relatives, teachers, and coaches. It can be a dangerous method of control that adults use, sometimes inadvertently and sometimes intentionally. By setting unreasonably high expectations and then showing disconnection and disapproval or anger if they are not met, an adult can induce a child to perform in the way that they want. This is a common scenario that often sets the stage for imposter syndrome to develop.

You can and should have expectations for your child, but these should be focused on their zone of proximal development (i.e., the next set of skills that they have to learn and improve on), which is individually focused and not focused on others, including your own wishes and desires. Being an adult often requires examining yourself and making sure that you are not imposing ideas that may be coming from maladaptive places. No matter what the outcome of your child's performance is, you should never shut them out emotionally or punish them in emotional ways. Love, affection, or attention should never be withheld for not meeting expectations. The damage you will cause to their relational functioning and performance issues will be long-lasting and hard for them to change.

POSITIVE, NEGATIVE, AND CONSTRUCTIVE FEEDBACK

To improve self-assessment and the ability to learn, you want your child to be strong in both receiving positive feedback and handling critical or constructive feedback. They should be able to take in that feedback following their performances. Positive feedback can be a real problem for those with impostor syndrome because they often feel like they are undeserving unless the performance was perfect, they handled it alone, or the person giving the feedback is deemed an authority. Positive feedback is so important for the ability to internalize success and accomplishment. Teaching your child how to take in compliments, praise, and positive words is a skill. You want to make sure that they are attending and fully present (i.e., making eye contact if possible and having an open posture) and acknowledging the comments by either receiving them through gratitude or some other acknowledgment. You should then teach them to integrate the comments into their understanding of their strengths, skills, and accomplishments.

Constructive feedback can be very difficult for children to acknowledge. Such feedback can be hard, especially when your child has perfectionistic expectations, as they can take the feedback personally (i.e., they take it to mean that they are bad people instead of focusing it on the behavior that they need to change) or they feel that there will be some negative consequence interpersonally as a result (e.g., they will lose connection with a person).

Teaching your child to separate the behavior from their individual self is important. Often, children can feel that getting constructive or critical feedback means that they themselves are "bad." Behavior is changeable, and we are constantly working on changing behavior. However, who your child is as an individual should not be what needs to change because that is seen as more constant and consistent. As an adult, you may sometimes have to take feedback your child receives and put it into a behavioral format or ask them to follow up with the person who gave the feedback to gather the behavioral feedback. You want your child to feel like constructive feedback is absolutely normal, and how they respond to it affects how much they can grow. You should model receiving constructive feedback in healthy ways and show them how you do it and how it benefits you. The way that your child works on constructive feedback is also important. They should see the value in working on the feedback and integrating it into their performance. They shouldn't believe that feedback should result in change immediately and recognize that a process may take time.

ANTs

Automatic negative thoughts (ANTs) can be present in many parts of the performance process. ANTs are usually irrational beliefs that immediately come into consciousness when you are in a triggering, stressful event. ANTs serve to diminish your confidence and abilities. To combat ANTs, you need a counter-argument. Teach your child how to challenge ANTs in various parts of the performance cycle and throughout their lifetime.

A few things are very important with ANTs. The first is identifying a thought as an automatic negative thought so your child can see it's a problem that requires some action on their part and not just a blanket belief. The second step is labeling the ANT (e.g., catastrophizing, fortune-telling) and understanding why it functions in the way it does. This helps your child externalize the ANT and seek proof to believe it. Finally, you must question the ANTs and look for evidence. Decide if it is true from the evidence you've gathered, and if it is not (which is usually the case), provide an alternative, reality-based, and positive response to the situation or trigger.

ANT LOG EXERCISE

Situation: I gave a speech in school.	
ANT: Emotional Reasoning	**Emotion Felt:** Embarrassment

ANT LOG EXERCISE

Your Response: It went badly. I didn't want to talk to anyone afterward.	**More Adaptive Response:** I could have asked my teacher for feedback to check my assumptions. I was very nervous.

AVOIDANCE

After a particularly difficult performance, a child might want to avoid participating in that type of performance again. But, as with academics, when a child refuses or does not want to go to school, it's important that they don't stop participating in something just because they did poorly. When a child refuses to go to school, it's typically important to understand why, but still have them attend school. The more that the trigger is avoided, the more of a problem it becomes. A difficult performance can teach a child that they can contend with frustration when things get hard, and in moments when they are not winning. They survive the experiences and learn from them. Returning to the performance arena fairly quickly is important so that the avoidance doesn't develop into a phobia.

If your child's avoidance is fraught with a lot of anxiety, it might be a great time to see a therapist, especially a cognitive behavioral therapist. These specialized therapists have research-backed strategies to help with avoidance-based anxiety so that your child can eventually try again.

KEY TAKEAWAYS

Hopefully, this chapter has built upon your knowledge and skills to address performance anxiety in an adaptive manner with your child, which includes:

- Understanding the important developmental aspects that you are trying to nurture in your child during an experience of performance anxiety (e.g., emotional regulation, performance expectations, healthy competition).
- Building skills to handle difficult performance moments, including dealing with ANTs, mental rehearsal, self-regulation, and mindfulness meditation.
- Being aware of your own expectations and how you must work on aspects of your own performance anxiety and management as a model for your child.

Chapter Five

PERFECTIONISM

The next stage of the Blooming phase is decreasing perfectionism. This chapter will cover the varying types of perfectionism, how to decrease it as a parental role model, the relationship between mental health concerns and perfectionism, nurturing a growth mindset, and obsessive-compulsive personality disorder (OCPD) and its link to perfectionism. Perfectionism is highly correlated to impostor syndrome, because if you are dealing with impostor syndrome, you believe you have no room to make mistakes or you will be revealed as a fraud. Perfectionism is highly correlated with impostor syndrome, and we tend to see it as underlying impostor syndrome.[16]

As a parent, it is critical that you teach your child to decrease perfectionism, even as they strive for greatness in their pursuits, in order to reduce the probability of them developing impostor

16 Linda E. Lee et al., "Perfectionism and the Impostor Phenomenon in Academically Talented Undergraduates," *Gifted Child Quarterly* 65, no. 3 (2021): 220–234, https://doi.org/10.1177/0016986220969396.

syndrome. Perfectionism may show up in two different ways in your child. In the first, they may overwork themselves to the point of exhaustion to ensure that their academic work product or their extracurricular activity results are perfect. In the second, they may procrastinate. Fearing that they will not be able to be perfect in delivering academic or extracurricular activity results, they wait until the last minute to provide a product or performance.

TYPES OF PERFECTIONISM

Perfectionism is defined as always evaluating oneself with rigid personal standards that refuse to accept anything less than perfection. Paul L. Hewitt and Gordon L. Flett describe three types of perfectionism in their multidimensional model of perfectionism:[17]

Self-oriented: Having impossibly high expectations of yourself, placing an unreasonable and unrealistic importance and pressure on yourself to be perfect, and being overly critical in your self-evaluation of your performance.

Socially prescribed: Believing that your family, friends, and colleagues are extremely demanding and will be overly harsh in their judgment of you if you are not perfect, and therefore, you must be perfect in order to secure and maintain their approval.

17 P. Hewitt and G. Flett, "Perfectionism in the Self and Social Context: Conceptualization, Assessment, and Association with Psychopathology," *Journal of Personality and Social Psychology* 60, no. 3 (March 1991): 456–70, https://doi.org/10.1037/0022-3514.60.3.456.

Other-oriented: Requiring unattainable standards of others and being overly critical of them.

Thomas Curran and Andrew Hill concluded in their 2017 study that all three types of perfectionism have increased over a twenty-seven-year period (1989–2016), suggesting that your child will face even greater perfectionism pressures than you may have as a child.[18]

SERVING AS A ROLE MODEL IN GIVING UP PERFECTIONISM

As a parent, you have an opportunity to serve as a role model to demonstrate how to give up perfectionism. In your own tasks and endeavors, you can easily slip into perfectionistic language and actions. If you make an error, you may automatically say out loud, "How could I be so stupid to make that mistake? That was totally unacceptable." If your child sees you beating yourself up for committing an error, then it is highly likely that they will do the same. You may also feel that perfectionism has made you successful, and you may be skeptical about the need to give it up. You may believe that it has made you work harder and be more focused. However, the costs of perfectionism, such as workaholism, anxiety and depression, strained relationships, and stress and burnout, tend to outweigh any perceived benefits. Further, there is no link between perfectionism and better performance. So, once you are able to give up perfec-

18 T. Curran and A. Hill, "Perfectionism Is Increasing Over Time: A Meta-Analysis of Birth Cohort Differences from 1989 to 2016," *Psychological Bulletin* 145, no. 4 (2019): 410–29, https://doi.org/10.1037/bul0000138.

tionism, you can serve as a great role model for your child to do so as well. Through your words and actions, you can model how to give up perfectionism.

HOW TO HELP YOUR CHILD GIVE UP PERFECTIONISM

In the process of relinquishing your own perfectionism, you can now teach your child how avoid it as a coping strategy. Here are some strategies to help your child give up perfectionism:

- **Be mindful of your language when providing feedback.** When your child shows you the result of a test, refrain from immediately asking, "Why didn't you get a perfect score?" Rather, explore with them what they may have gotten wrong and how much they understand why they got those answers incorrect. Also, highlight the things that they did understand and praise that. If they discuss their performance in an extracurricular activity such as sports, rather than say, "Why didn't you win?" you can ask, "What did you do well and what could you do better next time?" Such wording frames their results as a chance to learn and to grow, rather than as a disappointment in the lack of getting the right result.
- **Remind them that perfectionism is not responsible for their success.** Your child may believe that being perfect at something is the reason behind any success they have achieved. By reminding them that it is their unique talents and skills, not perfectionism, that are responsible for their success, it will be easier for them to give it up.
- **Help them accept the fact that the benefits of perfectionism do not outweigh its costs.** Reiterate that the costs of perfec-

tionism (e.g., anxiety and depression, burnout, etc.) do not outweigh its perceived benefits.

- **Emphasize that they should strive for greatness, not perfection.** In their academic pursuits or extracurricular activities, prompt your child to strive for greatness, meaning above average performance, but not to pursue perfection, because it is an impossible task, bound to lead to disappointment and failure.
- **Assist them in adopting a growth mindset.** A growth mindset will help your child be more resilient and have the resources to give up perfectionism. You may tend to adopt a fixed mindset without even being aware of it, which can influence how your child understands how to deal with challenges. When you say something such as "I am just not a numbers person, so my boss does not give me quantitative projects because I will make too many mistakes," it may signal a fixed mindset. Therefore, you want to be mindful of how you discuss your own views on how best to approach difficult situations, where you may not be perfect. Helping your child to view mistakes not as something to be avoided but rather as a chance to learn and grow will go a long way toward aiding them in giving up perfectionism.

RELATIONSHIP BETWEEN MENTAL HEALTH CONCERNS AND PERFECTIONISM

While you may view perfectionism as harmless, there is a link between perfectionism and mental health concerns such as depression, anxiety, eating disorders, or obsessive-compulsive disorder.[19] For instance, Wang and colleagues found that perfectionism predicted social anxiety, and perceived stress could explain the relationship between perfectionism and social anxiety.[20] Handley and her colleagues found a strong association between perfectionism, pathological worry, and generalized anxiety disorder.[21] Thus, it is crucial that you aid your child in giving it up to reduce the probability of serious mental health issues developing.

OBSESSIVE-COMPULSIVE PERSONALITY DISORDER AND PERFECTIONISM

The development of such rigid adherence to perfectionism into adulthood can becomes part of a child's personality, how they see themselves and relate to the world. This can result in the development of obsessive-compulsive personality disorder (OCPD). According to the *Diagnostic and Statistical Manual of Mental Disorders, Fifth Edition, Text Revision (DSM-5-TR)*, the standard use by mental health providers, the following

19 Thomas Callaghan et al., "The Relationships between Perfectionism and Symptoms of Depression, Anxiety, and Obsessive-Compulsive Disorder in Adults: A Systematic Review and Meta-Analysis," *Cognitive Behaviour Therapy* 53, no. 2 (2024): 121–32, https://doi.org/10.1080/16506073.2023.2277121.

20 Y. Wang et al., "The Relationship between Perfectionism and Social Anxiety: A Moderated Mediation Model," *International Journal of Environmental Research and Public Health* 19, no. 19 (2022): 12934, https://doi.org/10.3390/ijerph191912934.

21 A. Handley et al., "The Relationships between Perfectionism, Pathological Worry and Generalised Anxiety Disorder," *BMC Psychiatry* 14 (2014): 98, https://doi.org/10.1186/1471-244X-14-98.

are symptoms of OCPD. Unlike obsessive compulsive disorder (OCD), which features rituals and obsessive thoughts, OCPD is defined more by rigidity, an obsession with order and details, and excessive perfectionism.

Perfectionism: An overwhelming need for things to be perfect, often leading to excessive time spent on tasks and difficulty completing projects. Perfectionism that hinders the completion of tasks.

Rigidity and Inflexibility: Rigidity in thinking and behavior; stubbornness; finding it challenging to adapt to new situations or accept others' viewpoints; a preoccupation with order and details that results in the person missing the point of an activity; excessive conscientiousness and inflexibility related to morality or values (not explained by one's culture or religion).

Control Issues: A strong desire to control situations, environments, and even the behavior of others, which often leads to conflict in relationships and work settings; inability to get rid of worn or worthless objects, even if they lack sentimental value.

Difficulty Delegating Tasks: Struggle with delegating tasks to others; fearing that others won't meet their exacting standards.

Excessive Attention to Detail: Excessive focus on details, rules, and schedules, so that they lose sight of the bigger picture, which can impair productivity and effectiveness.

Procrastination: Delay in starting or completing tasks out of fear that they won't do them perfectly.

Difficulty Expressing Emotions: Trouble expressing their emotions so they seem detached or overly formal, which can strain personal relationships.

Struggles with Work-Life Balance: Prioritizing of work and productivity over leisure and relationships, often leading to burnout and social isolation; reluctance to delegate tasks to or work with others unless things are done their way.

Obsessive-compulsive personality disorder (OCPD) and impostor syndrome can intertwine in complex ways, often exacerbating each other. Individuals with OCPD tend to have an intense focus on perfectionism, which is a core aspect of both issues. This relentless pursuit of flawlessness can feed into impostor syndrome, where the person constantly feels inadequate despite evidence of their competence. The perfectionistic tendencies of someone with OCPD may lead them to set impossibly high standards for themselves, and when they inevitably fall short, they may feel like a fraud, doubting their abilities and fearing that others will see through their perceived shortcomings.

In professional or academic settings, this combination can be particularly debilitating. A person with OCPD might obsess over details, spending an excessive amount of time perfecting their work. Despite the high quality of their output, they might still feel that it's not good enough, driving them deeper into the belief that they don't truly deserve their success. This can create a vicious cycle where their impostor syndrome is fueled by the unrealistic expectations set by their OCPD, leading to chronic self-doubt and anxiety. The fear of being exposed as an impostor might also cause them to avoid taking on new challenges or responsibilities, further limiting their personal and professional growth.

Moreover, the rigid and controlling nature of OCPD can make it difficult for individuals to accept praise or recognition, as they may believe that their success is due to luck or external factors rather than their own capabilities. This reinforces the impostor syndrome, as they struggle to internalize their achievements. The combination of OCPD and impostor syndrome can lead to significant stress, burnout, and dissatisfaction, as these individuals are trapped in a cycle of striving for perfection while constantly feeling unworthy.

PARENTING TO PREVENT OCPD

To help prevent the development of OCPD in children, parents should focus on fostering a healthy balance between discipline and flexibility in their parenting approach. One key strategy is to encourage and model a growth mindset, which we discussed in early chapters, rather than an emphasis on perfectionism. Instead of setting rigid, high standards and focusing solely on the outcome, parents should praise the effort and process their children engage in.

Another important technique is to create an environment where flexibility and adaptability are valued. Parents should avoid imposing overly strict rules or schedules that leave little room for spontaneity or change. Instead, they can teach their children how to adapt to new situations and challenges by being open to alternative solutions and embracing unexpected outcomes. For instance, if plans change or something doesn't go as expected, parents can use it as an opportunity to discuss how to handle these situations with a positive attitude. This approach helps children develop resilience and reduces the likelihood of them becoming overly rigid or controlling in their behaviors and thought patterns.

Lastly, parents should be mindful of their own behavior and how it influences their children. This includes demonstrating how to cope with stress and disappointment without resorting to perfectionism or excessive control. Parents can show their children that it's okay to ask for help, to take breaks when needed, and to acknowledge when they're feeling overwhelmed. By modeling these behaviors, parents teach their children that it's okay to be imperfect, and that self-compassion and flexibility are crucial components of mental well-being.

Here's a creative list of things you can do with your kids to combat perfectionism actively:

- **Celebrate Mistakes as Learning Opportunities:** Encourage children to see mistakes as valuable learning experiences by discussing what can be learned from each mistake and how it helps them grow. Find a special celebration ritual for mistakes.
- **Model Imperfection:** Handle your own imperfections gracefully. Laugh at your mistakes and talk about what you learn from them to normalize the experience of being imperfect.
- **Create "Failure" Days:** Designate days where everyone in the family shares something they tried and failed at, celebrating the effort rather than the outcome.
- **Encourage Creative Play without Rules:** Provide opportunities for unstructured play, where there are no right or wrong ways

to do things, such as painting, building with blocks, or creating stories.

- **Set Realistic Expectations:** Help children set realistic goals by considering what has been attained in the past and what would be a realistic next step. Break down big tasks into manageable steps and emphasize progress rather than perfection.
- **Practice Mindfulness Together:** Engage in mindfulness activities that teach children to stay present and enjoy the process rather than worrying about achieving a perfect outcome.
- **Introduce Books and Stories on Overcoming Perfectionism:** Read and discuss books that feature characters who overcome perfectionism or learn to value effort and growth over perfection.
- **Create a "Bravery Jar":** Each time your child takes a risk or tries something new, add a note to a jar celebrating their bravery, focusing on their willingness to try rather than the result.
- **Encourage a Variety of Interests:** Expose your child to a wide range of activities and interests to prevent them from fixating on being perfect in just one area.

KEY TAKEAWAYS

- **Role of Parents in Mitigating Perfectionism:** You play a critical role in helping your children decrease perfectionism by serving as role models. By giving up your own perfectionistic tendencies and demonstrating self-compassion, you can guide your children in adopting healthier attitudes toward their pursuits.

- **Impact of Perfectionism on Mental Health:** Perfectionism is not harmless; it is strongly associated with mental health concerns such as anxiety, depression, and obsessive-compulsive disorder (OCD). This highlights the importance of addressing perfectionistic behaviors early to prevent long-term psychological effects.
- **Nurturing a Growth Mindset:** Encouraging children to adopt a growth mindset, where mistakes are seen as opportunities for learning rather than failures, is crucial in helping them overcome perfectionism. This mindset fosters resilience and reduces the fear of imperfection.
- **Practical Parenting Techniques:** Parents can prevent perfectionism by creating an environment that values flexibility, adaptability, and realistic expectations. This includes modeling imperfection, celebrating mistakes as learning opportunities, using creative techniques, and encouraging a variety of interests.

Chapter Six

COPING WITH FAILURE AND DISAPPOINTMENT

The final step of the Blooming stage is coping with failure and disappointment, which includes internal vs. external approval, redefining failure, being able to appreciate learning, and failure to launch. Whether it is in their academic pursuits or extra-curricular activities, as a parent, you never want your child to fail. However, failure is a natural part of one's developmental process. Therefore, it is critical that you are able to teach your child how to cope with failure and disappointment. The following anecdote gives you an example of a common failure situation that can arrive and what the parents discuss and when in the process of the experience.

TAMARA'S LOSS

Tamara is a nine-year-old swimmer. She loves the sport and would always win when she raced her friends in the pool. Her parents decided to register her for a local youth swim meet. Tamara was very excited and expected to win as she usually did against her friends. However, after placing tenth in her first meet, Tamara was visibly upset and threw a tantrum, crying loudly and complaining about the event and that she felt that she was treated unfairly. She told her parents that she hated it and she didn't want to compete any longer. Her parents attempted to calm her down at the pool and after that was unsuccessful, they said that they would speak to her further when they got home. After arriving home and giving Tamara some time to calm down, her parents sat her down and talked to her about how to deal with losing, how to handle failure, ways to think about the experience, and what she might need to feel like she could compete more successfully in the future.

PROPER COPING WITH FAILURE

Although failure can be extremely unsettling to your child, learning how to properly cope with it builds resilience, as well as a lack of fear of, and humiliation from, the experience. Here are some key components to assisting your child to coping with failure in a healthy manner:

- **Determine the best timing for this discussion.** Your child may not be ready to talk about their feelings immediately after the failure experience, especially if they feel overwhelmed by their emotions. Therefore, you may want to give them some time to return to a calmer state for the conversation. Once they are ready to have the discussion, you can explore their feelings.
- **Allow them to name the feeling first.** Do not assume that you know what it is. If they have trouble doing so, then you can help them by asking a question such as "I wasn't sure what you were feeling about losing. I thought it might be sadness, anger, frustration, or maybe a combination. What do you think it was?" Such framing allows your child to identify their own experience and provides you an opportunity to also give your perspective of what you observed from them. This is such an important part of the process of coping with failure because it can be challenging for them to understand how their feelings can contribute to their overall response to failure. That is, if they are angry, your child may want to lash out at you, their competitor, or any others involved in the experience (e.g., judge, coach, teacher). As a parent, your job is to help them name the specific feeling (e.g., anger, sadness), and to identify a more appropriate response (e.g., rather than lashing out, discussing what made them angry, how to express those feelings appropriately, and what they may need to calm them down).
- **Discuss their feelings and thoughts about the failure experience.** Tamara's parents asked her how it made her feel to place tenth in the swim meet. She told them it made her feel angry, embarrassed, and sad because she always wanted to win. Tamara's parents acknowledged her feelings and empa-

thized with her, saying how hard it is to have that experience and they understand that she wants to win. They also told her that having those feelings is understandable, and they appreciated her talking to them about it.

The chart on page 117 will help you begin to discuss emotional vocabulary. There are clearly a ton of words to capture feelings, and this is just meant to be a starting place.

- **Talk about how the feeling influenced their behavior.** If your child was angry after the failure experience and behaved very aggressively toward you or others (e.g., throwing things, yelling, etc.), you may want to point out how such behavior is not healthy or appropriate while also acknowledging their right to have such feelings.
- **Help them identify healthier responses in the future.** If your child talked about feeling out of control when they are angry, sad, or disappointed, you may want to explore how they could bring themselves back to a calm, baseline level by doing some breathing exercises or by simply counting backwards from 10, until they feel calm. Box breathing is one breathing method that your child can utilize, wherein they breathe in through their nose for a count of four, hold the breath for a count of four, breathe out through their nose for a count of four, and hold for a count of four. It is called box breathing because as you count to four each time, you envision drawing a box at each interval. It may take several attempts until you find the strategy that works for your child. So do not be discouraged if it takes some time before you land on the best approach.

EMOTION VOCABULARY

JOY	SURPRISE	SADNESS
Proud	Confused	Devastated
Excited	Astonished	Depressed
Hopeful	Startled	Guilty/Ashamed
Giddy	Stunned	Hurt
Passionate	Bewildered	Apathetic
Optimistic	Alarmed	Discouraged
Cheerful	Horrified	Powerless
Content	Shocked	Despondent
Comfortable	Puzzled	Indifferent
Free	Speechless	Anguished
ANGER	**FEAR**	**DISGUST**
Envious	Jealous	Resentful
Hostile	Nervous	Disappointed
Frustrated	Dread	Bitter
Defensive	Inadequate	Loathing
Aggressive	Vulnerable	Revolted
Tense	Anxious	Critical
Irritated	Hopeless	Bitter
Annoyed	Embarrassed	Irritated
Furious	Worried	Cynical
Disrespected	Panicked	Contempt

- **Normalize the failure experience while striving for future success.** Tamara stated that she thought that if she didn't win every swim meet, it meant she was not a good competitive swimmer. Her parents informed her that the nature of many sports, including swimming, is that you may first lose a great deal before you are able to win. It is a normal developmental process, where through experience and practice, you learn the strategies needed to win consistently. When Tamara heard this explanation, she felt relieved because she loved to swim and was concerned that she would not be able to continue if she was considered a "bad" competitive swimmer. Her parents told her that working with her coach would help her to get stronger in order to be more competitive in future meets. While the goal may not be for your child to get used to constant failure, normalizing the experience provides an opportunity for both you and your child to see the learning and appreciate the likelihood and necessity of failing.
- **Explore how they can learn from the failure experience.** It is human nature to stay stuck on the experience of failure so that we are unable to explore what learning took place from it. Speak to your child about what they learned from the experience. When Tamara's parents questioned her about what she learned from losing the swim meet, she asserted that she needed to practice more, that she did not get off to a good start, and she felt exhausted during the last laps of the meet. Tamara's parents were able to take this information and set up more practice time for her, informed her coach about how to help her get out of the starting blocks faster, and found a trainer for her to work on her conditioning.

- **Set up realistic expectations for future experiences.** While the goal is not to constantly focus on the failure experience, it is critical that your child reflect on it. This can help them to develop realistic expectations for future experiences. Tamara's parents discussed her expectations for her next swim meet. Tamara initially asserted that she wanted to win her race. While her parents did not dismiss this goal, rather than solely focus on winning the race, they encouraged her to set a goal for improving her time from the last swim meet.

INTERNAL VS. EXTERNAL APPROVAL

Especially early on, when your child deals poorly with failure, it is out of their concern about losing approval from you or other significant figures in their lives (e.g., teacher, coach). Impostor syndrome tells them they are not good enough and that they need external validation or approval to support any notion that they can be successful. When you overcome impostor syndrome, you are able to provide internal approval to yourself and identify the good things you have done well, rather than focusing on the things which you did wrong. As a parent, your goal is to help them understand the difference between internal approval versus external approval.

EXTERNAL APPROVAL

A child focused on external approval seeks to meet the expectations of someone other than themselves. They may have difficulty regulating themselves when they fail at a given task, fearing that they will lose the external approval they crave. As a parent, you must be mindful of not appearing to withhold your love and approval when your child may fail at a task or situation. While you may have your own experience of disappointment, you should first be aware of your child's needs when they fail at a specific task. As such, you should model how to handle failure in such a way that your child does not feel they have lost your approval. This may mean acknowledging your disappointment in their lack of success and communicating your pride in their effort. Rather than focus on everything they did wrong, which may have led to the failure experience, you can first examine the areas in which they excelled or improved. For instance, if your child lost their most recent tennis match, instead of talking immediately about what they did wrong in the match, explore with them what they did well, and if they have trouble identifying something, you can assist them by pointing out several things. Then you can explore what they could improve during their next match. This communicates that your love and care for them is not contingent on showing your external approval of their efforts or results.

INTERNAL APPROVAL

As a parent, you want your child to be able to bolster their self-confidence with internal approval, or the ability to provide positive feedback to themselves. When you child is not as successful as they might want to be or fails at a task or a situation, internal approval enables them to still maintain a sense of positive self-worth regarding their abilities. As a parent, here are some strategies to help your child develop and sustain their internal approval:

- **Help your child to maintain a positive internal voice.** When an individual is dealing with impostor syndrome, at the moment they experience failure or make a mistake, automatic negative thoughts are activated, which diminish their skills and sense of self. For instance, if your child makes an error during a piano performance, the Mind-reading ANT may tell them that everyone believes they are a terrible pianist. Help your child to develop a more positive internal voice, to counter these ANTs. For instance, when your child makes a mistake, you can teach them to think, "It's okay to make a mistake; you're human. Overall, you did well in your performance."
- **Provide clear examples of their skills and abilities.** Help your child to recognize, and subsequently internalize, their skills and abilities. For instance, if they tell you they performed poorly during a recent class group presentation, you can point out the fact that they have great communication skills, leadership, and organizational skills.
- **Model internal approval and a positive inner voice.** As a parent, you may be a harsh critic of not only your child, but of yourself. Therefore, it may be extremely challenging for you to model internal approval or a positive voice. However, by providing clear examples of internal approval and a positive voice for your child, you will enable them to realize how best to respond when they encounter a failure experience. For instance, if your child overhears you having a trying time on a client meeting, rather than say, "I really botched this client meeting today," you might instead share, "My client meeting today was full of wins and some losses. I think that I effectively discussed the client's needs and how we are addressing them. I also gave clear timelines on our deliverables, which really

pleased the client. I think that I could have done a slightly better job explaining our projections with the client. There was some room for improvement, but overall, I think I did a good job." Such modeling will also provide clear language for your child regarding how to best positively reinforce their achievements.

REDEFINING FAILURE

According to the *Merriam-Webster Dictionary*, failure is defined as "a lack of success."[22] For many, failure is something to be avoided at all costs, and it makes them feel ashamed. Teaching your child that failure does not have to be a shameful experience but one in which they learn new skills or approaches will be essential to their overall approach to dealing with failure in a healthy manner. Discussing the failure experience with your child allows them to understand how normal it is, which results in them being able to manage it better and to explore it with you differently. Here's an example of a supportive response to failure:

Jan is a 14-year-old female who is generally an outstanding student. She never received less than an A in any of her classes. However, recently, as Jan entered high school, she had some trouble with her algebra course. For the first time in her academic life, she received a failing grade on a quiz. Jan was greatly upset about it and attempted to hide it from her parents. She believed they would be ashamed of her because they always

22 Merriam-Webster, "Failure," *Merriam-Webster.com Dictionary*, accessed August 2, 2024.

talked about the importance of academic achievement. When she failed a second quiz, Jan became very despondent. Her mother noticed her change in demeanor and asked her what might be bothering her. Even though she was afraid to confide in her mother, she told her about the two failed algebra quizzes. Jan was surprised when her mother told her that she had the same experience with algebra and that she understood her difficulty. Jan's mother discussed how it is a usual occurrence to have some trouble with new subjects, especially with math. Failure of this sort did not mean she was stupid or unable to handle math. Instead, it meant that she might need more assistance in learning the concepts. Rather than being disappointed or ashamed of her, her parents were very supportive and decided to hire a tutor to help Jan with her algebra class.

GROWTH MINDSET

Teaching your child how to adopt a growth mindset will help them to be more resilient and have the resources to deal with failure experiences, when they encounter them. They will not internalize the experience as them being a failure but rather recognize that it is a normal part of growing and a chance to learn.

THE CONCEPT OF FAILING FORWARD

Failing forward is recognizing that any failure is part of the path to future successes. The notion is prevalent in a variety of industries, especially the tech sector. Many tech founders are more than happy to discuss how much they have failed, viewing it as a badge of honor. In their estimation, these failures contributed to their current achievements. When talking about failure with your child, it is helpful to explain that failure does not take place in a vacuum. Rather it is part of a larger story for their future accomplishments.

THE SELF-SABOTAGE CYCLE AND THE FAILURE TO LAUNCH

You may find yourself in a situation where you feel like your adult child has failed to launch. That is, in your estimation, your child has not been able to fully realize their potential and skills, to pursue a productive path, either academically or vocationally. If this may be your reality, there are a few things to consider. First, while you may believe that your child is lazy or unmotivated, it may be that they are experiencing the self-sabotage cycle, which is indicative of someone dealing with impostor syndrome. They may go through the impostor syndrome cycle II, as discussed in Chapter Four, where they worry about a performance (e.g., an academic test or a work project), self-sabotage by procrastinating, and when they receive a mixed or good review, rather than feel relieved, they begin to worry about the next performance. As a result, your child, who may appear to be unfocused and indecisive, might be struggling with the self-sabotage cycle.

Another aspect of impostor syndrome is perfectionism, discussed earlier, because an individual dealing with it believes that the only way to not be seen as a fraud is to never make a mistake. The perfectionism may make your child feel like if they cannot do something perfectly, a job or an academic program, they would rather not do it at all. This can lead to a complete avoidance of anything hard or perceived as difficult, which can show itself by underperforming, accomplishing less than expected or completely opting out of achieving anything.

Therefore, you can support your child by helping them to identify self-sabotage behaviors and perfectionism by understanding these potential root causes and teaching them that rather than avoiding there are other things that they can do to address it. These behaviors include:

- Managing the performance anxiety that precedes the self-sabotage through mindfulness activities and tools
- Breaking up the tasks they were avoiding into smaller, more manageable pieces
- Learning task management strategies like the Pomodoro technique
- Restructuring ANTs

THE IMPACT OF NEURO-DIVERGENCE ON FAILURE TO LAUNCH

Another reason that your child may have difficulty launching is due to an undiagnosed neurodivergence such as attention deficit hyperactivity disorder (ADHD) or autism spectrum disorder. If you find that your child has had difficulty maintaining focus, seems to lack attentional resources to complete tasks, or has been unable to maintain employment or an academic program, you may want to consider having them evaluated by a neuropsychologist. These are typical signs of an individual who may have ADHD, which features difficulty focusing, being easily distracted, and having challenges with task completion.

ADHD

According to the *DSM-5-TR*, the following are symptoms of ADHD:[23]

Inattention

- Fails to give close attention to details or makes careless mistakes in schoolwork, at work, or in other activities
- Has trouble holding attention on tasks
- Does not seem to listen when spoken to directly
- Has trouble organizing tasks and activities
- Often avoids, dislikes, or is reluctant to do activities that require mental effort over a long period of time
- Often loses things necessary for tasks and activities (e.g., keys, phone, glasses)
- Is easily distracted
- Is often forgetful in daily activities

Hyperactivity-Impulsivity

- Often fidgets with or taps hands or feet
- Talks excessively
- Has trouble waiting their turn

23 American Psychiatric Association, *Diagnostic and Statistical Manual of Mental Disorders: DSM-5-TR** 5th ed., Washington, DC: American Psychiatric Association, 2022, "Attention-Deficit/Hyperactivity Disorder," 59–66.

- Often interrupts or intrudes on others (e.g., interrupts conversations, etc.)

AUTISM SPECTRUM DISORDER[24]

Some symptoms of ASD include:

- Difficulty in communication with others at home, school, and work
- Trouble in reciprocal conversation; failure to respond in interactions or initiate them
- Struggles with nonverbal communication like eye contact, body language, facial expressions
- Trouble developing and sustaining relationships; indifference to peers and difficulty with imaginative play with others
- Repetitive motor movements (e.g., putting toys in particular order, mimicking and repeating what others say, flapping arms)
- Inflexible with routines, patterns, and verbal and nonverbal behavior and distress when they cannot engage in them (e.g., eating the same breakfast, rigid thinking, difficulty with transitions)
- Fixated interests (e.g., preoccupation with certain objects, obsessive focus on particular interests)
- Strong reactivity to sensory experiences (e.g., irritability with certain materials and tags, sounds, textures) and also a lack of reaction to others (e.g., indifference to pain)

24 American Psychiatric Association, *Diagnostic and Statistical Manual of Mental Disorders: DSM-5-TR* 5th ed., Washington, DC: American Psychiatric Association, 2022, "Autism Spectrum Disorder," 53–58.

While you may notice these symptoms in your child, it is important to note that a mental health professional should provide a diagnosis of neurodivergence, as other mental health disorders may account for some of these behaviors. If your child is diagnosed as neurodivergent, you may feel defensive or somehow responsible or blamed. However, it is important to understand that you did nothing wrong, you should not be ashamed or embarrassed, and the true focus should be on how best to help your child. If your child is neurodivergent, they can certainly thrive with the assistance of psychological interventions such as therapy or social skills groups, and possibly, medication, especially if they are diagnosed with ADHD.

MENTAL HEALTH CONSIDERATIONS WITH FAILURE TO LAUNCH

As discussed above, your child may not be neurodivergent but instead be dealing with another mental health condition, such as depression or anxiety, which may impact their failure to launch. For instance, if your child is depressed, they may not be able to summon up the energy to pursue tasks such as a job search or completing an academic degree. If your child is anxious, they may feel overwhelmed by the tasks required to secure a job or enroll in an academic program, or to identify another path for themselves. Therefore, it is essential that you are able to differentiate their specific concern so they may get the most effective treatment possible. It is also important to discuss your concerns with your child in the most supportive way possible. Rather than talking about your disappointment in their inability to launch, explore with them your belief in their potential, and your desire to help them better understand what might be stopping them from pursuing a specific path. By having this discussion, you can help them to recognize their strengths, current challenges, and interventions, which can aid them in achieving their goals.

KEY TAKEAWAYS

- **Coping with Failure Strategies:** You can help your child to deal with failure by modeling it, providing a context for failure (i.e., a natural part of anyone's path to success), and giving your child multiple coping strategies.
- **Noticing Self-Sabotage:** Recognize self-sabotage and how it can affect your child and its potential connection to perfectionism, then address it by dealing with the root causes and blockers that you can affect.
- **Failure to Launch Can Be Addressed:** Recognizing the factors (e.g., neurodivergence, mental health issues such as anxiety) which may be contributing to your child's failure to launch and how to address them, is critical to helping them to thrive.

Chapter Seven

INTERNALIZING SUCCESS

The final phase of the three B's model is Being, in which your child learns how to internalize success, recognizes the need to develop a self-care practice to regulate emotion and avoid burnout, and focuses on developing community. This chapter will explore how to help your child appreciate incremental growth, allow for celebration, even for small wins, and take in complicated wins. The chapter emphasizes the importance of recognizing one's own skills and efforts as the primary drivers of success, rather than attributing achievements to luck or external factors. By adopting these practices, you can help your child develop a healthy self-concept, reduce the risk of impostor syndrome, and nurture resilience.

THE MEANING OF INTERNALIZING SUCCESS

In order to help your child internalize their success, it will be important that you understand what that means. Internalizing success means:

- Attributing accomplishments to your own skills and talents
- Recognizing that your effort and hard work have enabled you to be successful
- Realizing that luck is not the main component of your progress

Helping your child to internalize their success will prevent impostor syndrome from controlling your child's narrative about themselves. Impostor syndrome wants your child to believe that their success is undeserved and is primarily through luck or a relationship with an important individual (e.g., teacher, coach) in their lives. By internalizing their success, your child will be able to lessen the influence of impostor syndrome in shaping their narrative.

IDENTIFYING/OWNING SKILLS AND STRENGTHS

A key part of internalizing success is being able to help your child identify and fully own their skills and strengths. In seeking to help your child develop and improve, you may primarily be focused on their areas for development while neglecting their key skills and strengths. However, it is important to assist your child in naming their areas of strength, so that they are able to fully appreciate how they contribute to their successes. Therefore, when your child achieves success at a given task or project, it will be vital for you to ask them to identify the skills and strengths that enabled them to do so. They may have trouble with this, and as a parent or caregiver, you can provide support. For instance, if your child performed well in a school play, you can discuss how their communication, organizational, and interpersonal skills aided in their success. By providing an opportunity for your child to identify their skills and strengths, you will allow them to internalize their success.

DEVELOPING AN ACCURATE SUCCESS NARRATIVE

A personal narrative is the story we tell ourselves about ourselves. These narratives are important because they can influence how we show up in the world and the sense of agency we have about impacting our own lives. Such narrative can include distortions, which do not accurately reflect our reality (e.g., "the only reason I have had any success is because people feel bad for me"). People who struggle with impostor syndrome often have such distorted narratives, which diminish their role in obtaining specific achievements. Therefore, when helping your child to internalize their success, it is crucial that you support them in developing an accurate success narrative, which includes objective information that will be difficult to distort (e.g., "I earned the highest grade in the class," "I finished first in my competition because

I won the most bouts"), and links it to factors tied to their own contributions (e.g. effort, specific skills).

DISMISSING LUCK AS THE SOLE REASON FOR SUCCESS

Some individuals, especially those dealing with impostor syndrome, may tend to attribute any success to luck or the result of a key relationship. However, in order to internalize success, it will be critical that you teach your child that luck is not the sole reason for their accomplishments. While in some circumstances, luck may be involved in a given success, clearly articulating how other factors (e.g., your child's skills, work ethic) played a more central role, will provide your child with accurate understanding of how they can have agency in most of their successes. Such an understanding will also enable them to internalize their success over the long term.

EMBRACING POSITIVE FEEDBACK

In order to fully internalize their success, your child must recognize how they played an active role in their accomplishments. This can be done through intentional self-reflection, where they think about their contributions to their success (e.g., strong work ethic, good leadership skills). And it can also be done by embracing positive feedback about their performance and their skills. Helping your child to embrace positive feedback, rather than deflect or dismiss it, as many individuals dealing with impostor syndrome tend to do, will give them another way to internalize their success in a healthy and proactive manner.

APPRECIATING INCREMENTAL GROWTH

What may be extremely challenging, especially for high-achieving parents, is to appreciate the incremental growth that is observed in your child. Your desire may be to see great leaps of development, whether it is in their academic performance or in their extracurricular activities. However, valuing incremental growth, and verbalizing your appreciation to your child, will help them to also recognize the importance of that growth. Let's take the example of Jeanine.

Jeanine is an eight-year-old girl who was having difficulty learning all her notes for her violin lessons. She often forgets various parts of a song and was unable to complete a song during her first recital. Jeanine's parents are extremely frustrated, especially because they have paid for violin lessons three times a week and believe that Jeanine should have exhibited faster growth. Jeanine senses her parents' disappointment and begins to feel like she will never be a good violinist. However, Jeanine's violin instructor has reported that during the last few lessons, she has noticed some small but clear signs of growth with Jeanine. She has been able to make it through most songs they practiced while only forgetting one or two notes. She also seems very much engaged with the songs, asking more questions about them, than she has ever done before. The report by Jeanine's violin teacher makes her parents realize that they were ignoring her incremental growth and only focused on seeing major leaps in her development. To appreciate incremental growth you should:

- **Set realistic expectations, tied to a reasonable time frame.** Although you may wish to see exponential growth in your child's performance, such major gains may not be realistic over a short period of time. For example, if your child has been receiving C's on their math quizzes, it may not be realistic to expect straight A's over the next marking period. Set measurable expectations that are linked to realistic timelines (e.g., a 10 percent increase in your child's grades over three marking periods).
- **Note even small signs of progress.** Rather than solely focusing on large steps in growth, recognize any sign of progress. For instance, if your child is so distracted and is usually unable to sit still for no more than five minutes to focus on their schoolwork, be sure to note the moment they are able to do so for six minutes or seven minutes.
- **Identify your child's current state vs. their previous state.** It is easy to neglect incremental growth because it can seem so subtle, to the point of being unnoticeable. If you take a moment to observe where your child was at one moment and where they are now, you will realize that they made important progress. For instance, if your child was constantly losing their fencing bouts by a score of 0 to 5 a month ago but is now losing 3 to 5 consistently, it is a sign of growth, albeit not yet where you want them to be in terms of achieving victories. It may feel tough to value incremental growth when you are so focused on the ultimate goal (e.g., high academic achievement or wins in a sport). However, by recognizing your child's incremental growth, you will aid them in grasping the progress they

have made, which will allow them to internalize the skills and efforts that made it possible.

- **Discuss the learning lessons from the growth experience.** When you observe incremental growth, it is also an opportunity to understand the learning lessons from the experience. What enabled your child to make such growth? What may be stopping them from further growth? How can you help them to continue to develop at a reasonable pace? In searching for answers, you will be able to better understand how to support your child.

ALLOWING FOR CELEBRATION

For some parents, allowing for celebration may seem like a distraction from the task or goal at hand. Therefore, when a child achieves a specific goal (e.g., getting an A on a test, first place in a sporting event, recognition for a great musical or theatrical performance), rather than celebrating that accomplishment, many parents simply focus on the next goal. This may be to ensure that their child does not become complacent, causing them to be too comfortable with the accomplishment, or possibly lose motivation. However, when you do not allow for celebration, your child is not able to fully appreciate how their skills, talents, and hard work contributed to their achievement. This may lead them to conclude that it was luck or an aberration. Allowing for celebration acknowledges both the achievement and the effort and skills that were required for it. It enables your child to recognize their strengths, while still understanding that there are areas for further development. It is not a distraction, and it will not make them complacent or lazy.

CELEBRATING EVEN SMALL WINS

You may reserve celebrations for huge victories. However, small wins are just as valuable for your child's growth and development. A small win is any event or situation where your child has incrementally achieved a goal, which can lead to an ultimate bigger accomplishment. Although some parents feel that the "everyone gets a trophy" mentality makes children less resilient and may be turned off by the concept, it is useful to understand that linking the small win to your child's efforts and ability reinforces their agency and counters any possible development of impostor syndrome.

For example, Jonathan is a nine-year-old boy who recently started playing soccer on a local youth club team. Jonathan has been in a reserve role since he joined the team, and at times, he does not even get into the game. However, during the last soccer match, his coach played Jonathan, who got two shots on goal, although he did not score. After the game, his coach told him that as a result of his hard work during practice, he intended to play Jonathan more and might even make him a starter. Even though his team was defeated in this match, Jonathan's parents viewed his entry into the game and the future possibility of playing more as small wins. Therefore, they took the time to celebrate them with Jonathan and reinforced the coach's words about the impact of his practice effort on the coach's views about his ability to contribute to the team.

TAKING IN COMPLICATED WINS

So how do you respond when your child has a win that is a bit complicated? This may be one in which things did not go as perfectly as planned. For example, if your child did well in a tennis tournament, winning more matches than ever before but made a great deal more unforced errors, they may feel like it was a disappointment and be unable to enjoy the experience. In these cases, help your child to appreciate the positive aspects of their win while also being able to examine the areas to further address. Taking in and valuing complicated wins will further aid your child in overcoming impostor syndrome since they will be able to internalize their skills, diminishing the automatic negative thoughts that tell them that they have no true abilities.

SUSTAINING THE INTERNALIZATION OF SUCCESS

Once you have assisted your child in internalizing their success, it will be critical to also help them to sustain it. When moments arise in which your child may wish to attribute a success to solely luck or having difficulty naming their unique skills and strengths, you can remind them of their role in their success and support them in identifying key skills. Sustaining the internalization of success can also protect your child from experiencing impostor syndrome, since many dealing with this issue are unable to own their success and oftentimes have a distorted narrative about their achievements. It will be essential for you to teach your child that sustaining the internalization of success is a lifelong process, on which they must continually work.

KEY TAKEAWAYS

- **Internalizing Success:** Teaching children to attribute their accomplishments to their own skills, talents, and efforts is essential for helping them internalize success and prevent impostor syndrome.
- **Identifying Key Skills and Strengths:** Helping your child to identify their unique skills and strengths will enable them to fully own their contributions, which have led to their successes.
- **Developing an Accurate Success Narrative:** By aiding your child in developing an accurate success narrative, it will help them to dismiss luck as a sole reason for their success, while also integrating objective measures for their success into this narrative.
- **Appreciating Incremental Growth and Small Wins:** Recognizing and celebrating even small signs of progress can help your child understand the value of incremental growth, fostering a sense of achievement and encouraging further development.
- **Setting Realistic Expectations:** You should set realistic expectations tied to reasonable timelines and allow your child to see measurable progress and avoid the pressure of achieving unrealistic goals.

- **Allowing for Celebration:** Celebrating achievements, whether big or small, helps your child appreciate their efforts and skills, reinforcing their sense of self-worth and countering the development of imposter syndrome.
- **Addressing Complicated Wins:** You should help your child appreciate the positive aspects of complicated wins, where not everything went perfectly, to ensure they can still internalize their successes and learn from what went wrong.
- **Sustaining the Internalization of Success:** As a parent, aiding your child in sustaining the internalization of their success will be a key factor in guarding against the development of impostor syndrome.

Chapter Eight

EMOTIONAL REGULATION AND BURNOUT PREVENTION

Having worked for years with clients who struggle with impostor syndrome, we have noticed that they often have terrible and neglectful self-care habits, which were never properly formed in childhood. The research backs this by showing a relationship between impostor syndrome and increased experiences of burnout.[25] Many of them grew up in family cultures where work-aholism was idealized and self-care nonexistent. We totally understand that we live in very driven and overworked cultures that extend far beyond work to school and extracurricular activities. We ask that you begin to create environments within your home that values and models self-care and burnout prevention.

And that begins with you...

---

25 Jennifer A. Villwock et al., "Impostor Syndrome and Burnout among American Medical Students: A Pilot Study," *International Journal of Medical Education* 7 (2016): 364–69.

When we discuss self-care, we are talking about behaviors that give you a sense of being replenished, filled up—maybe not all the way to the top, but more than before you did the activity. For your children to respect the importance of self-care in their lives, they are going to have to see you live it and benefit from it as well. So, honestly assess how the adults in your household take care of themselves, engage in self-care, and handle episodes of overwhelm and burnout. What self-care behaviors do you engage in? Or do you have any at all? How do you discuss feelings of exhaustion and tiredness with your children? Or do you not discuss it? How do they know when you are at your limit? Is it shown in negative ways, such as irritability and a short fuse? What happens when you are burned out? How do you handle it? Do you handle it intentionally or just hope for it to go away? Probably the single, most important component of instilling this in your child is how you deal with it yourself.

THE FOUNDATION OF SELF-CARE: UNDERSTANDING AND MODELING BALANCE

Self-care is not just about occasional indulgences or temporary escapes from the stressors of life. It's a comprehensive approach to living that prioritizes balance, well-being, and sustainability in our daily lives. It's about finding a rhythm that allows us to meet our responsibilities while also maintaining our physical, emotional, and mental health.

Children learn by observation. They first learn by watching the adults around them, and this applies to your self-care regimen. If they see that you prioritize work above all else, they will likely adopt the same habits. However, if they witness you engaging in regular self-care practices—whether that's setting aside time for exercise, meditation, pursuing hobbies, maintaining social connections, or simply resting when needed—they will begin to understand that taking care of oneself is an essential part of life, not an afterthought.

Start by assessing how you balance your work, family life, and personal time. Are you constantly pushing yourself to the brink of exhaustion? Do you regularly sacrifice your well-being to meet external demands? Or do you make it a point to carve out time for activities that replenish your energy and bring you joy? Reflecting on these questions can help you identify areas where you might need to make changes, not only for your own benefit but also to set a positive example for your children.

It's not enough to simply engage in self-care practices; you must also communicate the importance of these activities to your children. Talk openly about why you take time for yourself and how it helps you manage stress and maintain your overall well-being. For instance, if you take a walk after dinner to clear your mind, explain to your children how this helps you feel more relaxed and refreshed. By doing so, you're teaching them that self-care is not selfish—it's necessary.

CREATING A HOME ENVIRONMENT THAT SUPPORTS SELF-CARE

Creating a home environment that prioritizes self-care requires a collective effort. It's about establishing routines, setting boundaries, and fostering a culture that values well-being over constant productivity. Here's how you can start:

ESTABLISHING ROUTINES

Routines provide structure and predictability, which can be incredibly comforting and stabilizing for both children and adults. When self-care becomes a regular part of your routine, it's easier to maintain even during stressful times. For example, you might establish a family routine where everyone spends an hour each evening doing something they enjoy—reading, drawing, listening to music, or simply relaxing. This not only helps each family member unwind, it also reinforces the idea that taking time for oneself is a normal and necessary part of life.

Another important routine to consider is sleep. Prioritizing sleep is a fundamental aspect of self-care, yet it's often the first thing sacrificed in our busy lives. Create a sleep-friendly environment in your home by setting consistent bedtimes, reducing screen time before bed, and ensuring that everyone has a comfortable and quiet place to sleep. Discuss the importance of rest and how it contributes to their health and ability to function well in school and other activities.

SETTING BOUNDARIES

Boundaries are essential for maintaining balance and preventing burnout. In the context of self-care, boundaries might involve setting limits on work hours, saying no to unnecessary commitments, or designating certain times of the day as "technology-free" to focus on more restorative activities. It's important to establish these boundaries not just for yourself, but also for your children.

Teach your children the importance of setting their own boundaries. They might need to limit the number of extracurricular activities they participate in or set aside time each day for unstructured play or relaxation. Encourage them to listen to their bodies and minds and to advocate for their needs when they feel overwhelmed or stressed. This empowers them to take control of their own well-being and prevents the kind of overextension that often leads to burnout.

FOSTERING A CULTURE OF WELL-BEING

Beyond routines and boundaries, fostering a culture of well-being in your home involves promoting values that support mental, emotional, and physical health. This might include:

- **Encouraging Open Dialogue:** Create a safe space where everyone feels comfortable discussing their feelings, stressors, and needs. Regular family check-ins can be a great way to gauge how everyone is doing and to offer support where needed.
- **Prioritizing Physical Health:** Physical activity, healthy eating, and regular medical check-ups should be normalized as part

of self-care. Encourage your children to engage in activities that they enjoy and that help them stay active and healthy.

- **Valuing Rest and Play:** Rest and play are often undervalued in our productivity-focused culture, but they are critical components of self-care. Ensure that there is time for both in your family's routine. Play is not just for young children; it's a way for people of all ages to decompress, connect with others, and find joy in the present moment.
- **Promoting Mindfulness and Relaxation:** Teach your children simple mindfulness techniques, such as deep breathing or guided imagery, to help them manage stress and stay grounded. Incorporate these practices into your daily life, whether through meditation, breathwork, yoga, or simply taking a few moments to breathe deeply and center yourself.

TEACHING CHILDREN TO RECOGNIZE AND PREVENT BURNOUT

It is a powerful gift to recognize when you are approaching burnout and know how to prevent it. Teach your kids to listen to their bodies, understand their limits, and prioritize their well-being. Furthermore, discuss the signs of burnout. Help them understand that feeling overwhelmed, irritable, or exhausted are indicators that it's time to slow down and reassess their needs. When they see you acknowledge and address your own limits, they'll learn to recognize and respect their own. This kind of transparency helps demystify the concept of self-care, making it an accessible and integral part of their lives.

RECOGNIZING THE SIGNS OF BURNOUT

Children may not always have the language to articulate their feelings of stress or overwhelm, so it's important to help them recognize the physical and emotional signs of burnout. These might include:

- **Physical Symptoms:** Headaches, stomachaches, fatigue, or changes in sleep patterns can all be indicators of stress or burnout.
- **Emotional Symptoms:** Increased irritability, anxiety, sadness, or feelings of helplessness are common emotional signs of burnout.
- **Behavioral Changes:** A child who is burnt out might withdraw from activities they usually enjoy, struggle to concentrate, or show a lack of motivation.

Encourage your children to check in with themselves regularly and to share how they are feeling with you or another trusted adult. This helps them develop self-awareness and ensures that they don't ignore the early signs of burnout.

TEACHING COPING STRATEGIES

Once children recognize the signs of burnout, they need effective strategies to cope with and prevent it. Some strategies you can teach include:

- **Time Management:** Help your children learn to prioritize their tasks and manage their time effectively. This might involve breaking tasks into smaller, manageable steps, setting realistic deadlines, and ensuring that they schedule regular breaks. The Pomodoro Technique, where you set aside time in 25-minute-interval blocks to just do one task, can be a simple and easy method that is quite effective.

- **Relaxation Techniques:** Introduce your children to various relaxation techniques, such as deep breathing, progressive muscle relaxation, or visualization. These can help them calm their minds and bodies when they start to feel overwhelmed.
- **Healthy Outlets:** Encourage your children to engage in activities that help them release stress in a healthy way, whether that's through physical activity, creative expression, or simply spending time in nature.
- **Seeking Support:** Demonstrate to your child that it is important to ask for help when you need it and celebrate and reward them when they do. Whether they're struggling with schoolwork, friendships, or personal challenges, they should know that they have a support system they can rely on.

ENCOURAGING SELF-COMPASSION

A critical aspect of preventing burnout is teaching children to be kind to themselves. Self-compassion involves treating oneself with the same care and understanding that we would offer to a friend in distress. When children learn to practice self-compassion, they are less likely to engage in constant self-criticism or push themselves to the point of exhaustion.

Model self-compassion by showing yourself grace when things don't go as planned. Speak kindly to yourself in front of your children, and let them see you practicing forgiveness and understanding with yourself when you make mistakes. Encourage them to do the same by reminding them that it's okay to be imperfect. Everyone has limitations.

REIMAGINING SUCCESS: SHIFTING FROM ACHIEVEMENT TO WELL-BEING

In many families, success is measured by achievements—grades, awards, accolades—rather than by overall well-being. However, this achievement-focused mindset can contribute to burnout and neglect of self-care. To counteract this, shift the focus from what your children accomplish to how they feel and function in their daily lives.

VALUING EFFORT OVER OUTCOME

With self-care, the development of consistent practices takes time, and the outcome is usually in retrospect after a significant period. For example, it's very common to think that one experience with meditation should be transcendent, but that is rarely the case. Those special experiences probably happen occasionally and when you have been practicing for a long time. Help your child recognize that immediate outcomes are not really the goal of putting self-care into place. It's really meant to make sure that your child prioritizes their well-being and provides themselves opportunities to take care of their mind and body.

CELEBRATING SMALL WINS

In our fast-paced world, it's easy to overlook small achievements in favor of bigger milestones. However, celebrating small wins can be incredibly motivating and affirming. When you notice your child is trying to commit to a routine even if it's not fully consistent yet, acknowledging the tiny ways in which they have made progress becomes very important. There are a lot of bumps along the road to developing practices that take care of yourself, but the ability to see the little wins in your process can continue to keep you motivated to go on.

INTEGRATING SELF-CARE INTO EVERYDAY LIFE

The final step in creating a self-care-focused home environment is integrating these practices into everyday life. Self-care shouldn't be seen as something that happens only when we're burnt out or stressed or when we have some time left over from our tough school or work responsibilities; it should be a regular, ongoing part of our routines. Here are some practical ways to weave self-care into your family's daily life:

MINDFUL MORNINGS

Start the day with mindfulness. Whether it's a few minutes of deep breathing, a short meditation, or simply sitting together in silence, mindful mornings can set a positive tone for the rest of the day. This practice helps everyone in the family feel centered and ready to take on the day's challenges with a calm and focused mindset.

FAMILY MEALS AS A SELF-CARE RITUAL

Family meals are a wonderful opportunity to practice self-care together. Use mealtime as a chance to reconnect, share your day, and enjoy nourishing food. Encourage everyone to put away their devices and be fully present. This not only strengthens family bonds but also reinforces the importance of taking time to slow down and appreciate the simple pleasures in life.

EVENING WIND-DOWN ROUTINES

Create a calming evening routine that helps everyone transition from the busyness of the day to a restful night's sleep. This could include activities like reading, journaling, or practicing gratitude. Teaching your children to wind down at the end of the day helps them establish healthy sleep habits and signals to their bodies that it's time to relax and recharge.

INCORPORATING PHYSICAL ACTIVITY

Physical activity is a crucial component of self-care. Encourage your family to move their bodies in ways that feel good, whether it's a walk in the park, a family bike ride, or a dance party in the living room. Exercise not only supports physical health but also boosts mood and reduces stress, making it an essential part of a balanced lifestyle.

CREATIVE EXPRESSION

Creative activities like drawing, writing, or playing music can be powerful forms of self-care. Encourage your children to explore their creative interests as a way to express their emotions and unwind. Creativity is not only a great stress reliever, but also a way to connect with oneself and find joy in the process of producing something new.

NATURE TIME

Spending time in nature is a simple yet effective way to practice self-care. Whether it's a family hike, a visit to a local park, or just sitting outside and listening to the birds, putting your feet on the grass, being in nature can help everyone feel more grounded and connected to the world around them. Nature has a unique ability to soothe our minds and bodies, making it an ideal setting for family self-care.

QUALITY SLEEP

Finally, prioritize quality sleep for everyone in the family. Sleep is the foundation of good health, and without it, all other aspects of self-care become much harder to maintain. Create a sleep-friendly environment at home by keeping bedrooms cool and dark, establishing regular bedtimes, and limiting screen time before bed. Teach your children the importance of sleep and how it helps them grow, learn, and feel their best.

EMOTIONAL REGULATION

Emotional regulation is a foundational aspect of overall development, as it equips children with the tools to navigate their feelings with resilience and confidence instead of fear or compartmentalization and bottling them up. For children, learning these skills is crucial, as it helps them handle difficult emotional situations, build positive relationships, and make sound decisions. Parents and caregivers are critical as they themselves model emotional regulation in real time and provide consistent guidance and support on how to do it successfully.

Help children identify and label their emotions. This process begins with encouragement to express feelings in words and providing a strong and rich vocabulary for emotions, which not only helps children understand their emotions but also normalizes the experience of having a wide range of feelings. For example, you might say, "It seems like you're feeling really frustrated right now. Can you tell me more about what's making you feel this way?" This exploration helps kids develop an extensive emotional vocabulary and a more complex and articulated understanding of their internal experiences.

The next step is teaching them healthy coping strategies. This might involve introducing them to techniques such as deep breathing, counting to ten, or taking a break to calm down when they feel overwhelmed. In essence, give them space to feel the emotion, but not to act on it, and then lower the intensity. You can also encourage your child to engage in activities that help them manage their emotions, like drawing, writing, or playing. It's important for children to learn that it's okay to feel upset or angry, but it's how they respond to these emotions that matters. By practicing these strategies in everyday situations, children can develop the ability to regulate their emotions more effectively over time.

When you handle your emotions calmly and constructively, you provide a living example for your children to emulate. For instance, if you are feeling stressed, you might say, "I'm feeling a bit stressed right now, so I'm going to take a few deep breaths to help myself calm down." This not only demonstrates how to manage emotions but also shows that it's normal to experience strong feelings and that there are healthy ways to cope with them.

Finally, it's important to recognize that teaching emotional regulation is an ongoing process that requires patience and reinforcement. Children may not always respond perfectly, and that's okay. What matters most is that they are gradually learning to understand and manage their emotions. Parents should celebrate small successes and continue to offer guidance as their children grow and face new emotional challenges. Over time, with consistent support, children will develop the emotional regulation skills they need to thrive both in childhood and beyond.

SELF-CARE AS A LIFELONG PRACTICE

One of the most important lessons you can impart to your children is that self-care is a lifelong practice. It's not something they can perfect overnight, nor is it a one-size-fits-all solution. Self-care will look different at various stages of life, and it's important to be flexible and adapt to changing needs and circumstances.

Encourage your children to view self-care as a journey rather than a destination. Help them understand that it's okay to try different approaches and find what works best for them. As they grow older, their self-care practices will evolve, and they'll need to learn to listen to their bodies and minds to determine what they need at any given time.

REVISIT SELF-CARE PRACTICES

Make it a habit to periodically revisit your family's self-care practices. What worked well last year might not be as effective now, and that's okay. Have regular discussions with your children about how they're feeling and whether their current self-care routines are meeting their needs. Be open to making adjustments and trying new things.

ENCOURAGE INDEPENDENCE

As your children grow, encourage them to take more responsibility for their own self-care. This doesn't mean you stop guiding them, but rather that you empower them to make their own choices about how they take care of themselves. Whether it's choosing their own bedtime, deciding how to spend their free time, or finding their own ways to relax, giving them this autonomy helps them build confidence and a sense of ownership over their well-being.

LEARNING FROM SETBACKS

Finally, teach your children that setbacks are a natural part of the self-care journey. There will be times when they fall out of their routines, get overwhelmed, or simply don't feel like taking care of themselves. These moments are opportunities for learning and growth. Help them understand that self-care is not about being perfect, but about being kind to themselves, even when things don't go as planned.

BUILDING A LEGACY OF SELF-CARE

By prioritizing self-care in your family, you're not only improving your own well-being but also creating a legacy that your children can carry with them throughout their lives. The habits, attitudes, and values you instill in them now will shape how they approach their own health and happiness in the future.

Remember, self-care is not a luxury—it's a necessity. It's the foundation upon which we build our lives, and it's essential for maintaining the energy, resilience, and joy that we need to thrive. By modeling and teaching self-care, you're giving your children the tools they need to navigate life's challenges with grace and confidence.

In a world that often glorifies busyness and productivity, choosing to prioritize self-care is a radical act of self-love. It's a statement that says, "I matter. My well-being matters." And when you teach your children this lesson, you're helping them build a life that is not just about surviving, but about thriving.

So, take a moment to reflect on how you can bring more self-care into your life and your family's life. Start small, be consistent, and most importantly, be gentle with yourself and your loved ones as you embark on this journey together. Self-care is a gift that keeps on giving, and by embracing it, you're laying the groundwork for a healthier, happier, and more balanced life for you and your children.

KEY TAKEAWAYS

- **Modeling Self-Care Is Crucial:** Your children learn about self-care by observing how you prioritize your own well-being. It's essential to actively engage in self-care practices and communicate their importance to your children.
- **Balance Work and Rest:** Establishing a balance between work, family responsibilities, and personal time is key to preventing burnout. Model this balance at home.
- **Communication about Well-Being:** Open communication about stress, exhaustion, and the need for self-care helps children understand that taking care of oneself is necessary and not a sign of weakness.
- **Routine and Structure:** Incorporate self-care, such as regular sleep schedules and time for relaxation, into daily routines. Normalize these practices and make them a consistent part of family life.

- **Boundaries Are Essential:** Teach your children the importance of setting limits to protect their well-being.
- **Recognizing Burnout Signs:** Teach your children to recognize the physical, emotional, and behavioral signs of burnout in themselves so they can take action before becoming overwhelmed.
- **Self-Compassion:** Encourage self-compassion during times of stress or failure, reducing the risk of burnout and promoting emotional resilience.
- **Redefining Success:** Shift the focus from achievement to well-being. This teaches children that success is not just about what they accomplish, but also about how they feel and function in their daily lives.
- **Emotional Regulation:** Teach your children to recognize, understand, and manage their emotions for their overall development. This process involves helping them identify their feelings, introducing healthy coping strategies, modeling emotional regulation as parents, and consistently reinforcing these skills over time.

Chapter Nine

COMMUNITY DEVELOPMENT

Impostor syndrome shows up directly in how people connect with others. It's especially impactful in how they relate when they need help and during difficult times. Those with impostor syndrome are often very good at keeping their struggles to themselves. This habit stems from childhood, when they felt this made them easier to deal with, felt there was no space for their struggles, and/or they didn't feel like they could consistently rely on others to show up for them. So, they are excellent at doing things alone, often to their own detriment (e.g., burnout, being known for poor collaboration). We often discuss this tendency as showing up as the "lone wolf."

With impostor syndrome, this lack of community is often thought of as a strength and a necessity. Full accountability for a success requires single-handedly delivering it, and the overwork this requires is a source of pride. It can be very difficult to break this perception after the distinct distrust built up over the years. The vulnerabilities of mistake-making and failure are hidden from anyone or revealed to a very select few. Preserving a particular image is undergirded by the fear of being a fraud and misconceptions around what success truly can mean (e.g., achievements that are flawed, learning even from failure). Letting people in can become a dangerous risk that may lead to exposing the perceived fraudulence.

The unrealistic expectations and perfectionism of those with impostor syndrome often impacts their relationships. They lose trust in others, who do not show up for them in the ways that they want or expect. This can make them less tolerant of mistakes in others and more likely to find easy excuses to perceive someone as unreliable or untrustworthy.

HEALTHY APPROACH TOWARD BUILDING RELATIONSHIPS

Creating, building, and maintaining community is fundamental for children's social and emotional development. When children understand that they are part of something bigger than just themselves, they actively learn skills and awareness related to collaboration, cooperation, conflict management, reciprocity, and connection through shared values. They also learn to appreciate diverse perspectives, develop empathy, and build relationships based on trust and respect. This foundation is crucial not only for their personal growth, but also for fostering a sense of belonging and security, which are vital components of healthy self-esteem.

In relation to impostor syndrome, a supportive community can play a pivotal role in helping children recognize and validate their own contributions and achievements. Children who actively participate in community-building activities, such as group projects, team sports, or volunteering, learn to see the value of collaboration and collective effort.[26] This understanding counters the isolating effects of impostor syndrome, where individuals may feel that their successes are undeserved or that they are deceiving others about their capabilities. By experiencing success as part of a team or community, children come to understand that collaborating with others does not diminish their personal achievements, but rather enhances them. This experience helps children internalize a more balanced view of their abilities and accomplishments.

A sense of agency and confidence grows when contributing meaningfully to group efforts. It encourages children to take initiative, share ideas, and lead in various capacities, knowing that their input is valued and respected. This active engagement helps children develop a robust self-concept, where they see themselves as competent and capable individuals. It also prepares them for future challenges by instilling a mindset that success can be a collaborative endeavor without compromising individual ownership of one's contributions. In this way, children learn that they can accomplish great things both independently

26 Carly B. Slutzky and Sandra D. Simpkins, "The Link Between Children's Sport Participation and Self-Esteem: Exploring the Mediating Role of Sport Self-Concept," *Psychology of Sport and Exercise* 10, no. 3 (2009): 381–89; Monica Luque-Suárez et al., "Promoting Emotional and Social Well-Being and a Sense of Belonging in Adolescents through Participation in Volunteering," *Healthcare* 9, no. (March 22, 2021): 359, doi:10.3390/healthcare9030359.

and with others, counteracting the self-doubt and insecurity associated with impostor syndrome.

VULNERABILITY IN RELATIONSHIPS

Many people struggling with impostor syndrome feel like they always have to be alright and have no hardships or needs. Because their family only accepted their positive achievements and expected them to be of help to others and easy to deal with, they can often feel like a burden or dismissed when they raise difficulties with other people. At the slightest hint of not being heard, they choose not to share, which can often leave them feeling alone in their circumstances.

Validating your child's feelings becomes a foundational experience for them of trusting others, especially when a child seems to be fine, good at handling big burdens and intense situations, and generally unproblematic. It can be easy to miss or ignore what can be going on with a child who seems to be doing well overall. However, that's often why people with impostor syndrome say, "I was doing well at school and not getting into trouble, so nobody noticed that I was struggling in other ways." That struggle might be anxiety, a learning disability that they are overworking to compensate for, or just overwhelm and insecurity, but it's important that you see it, explore it, and allow it to be present, then support ways to address it.

Being told, "How can that be, you are so smart and capable, you need to get over it" and generally being dismissed after confiding of struggle can feel very shameful for someone with imposter syndrome and can increase the feeling of something being wrong with them. You don't want to mimic that experience for your child. Instead, make sure that they feel seen. Know that they can be both good with others and emotionally struggle. They can find things hard and still be smart, make mistakes, and be capable. Letting your child feel vulnerable with you and know that you can hold that and still value them becomes so important for their future.

With impostor syndrome, the self-sabotage coping cycle is common. As children, these adults weren't getting it right. They were seen as a screw-up, lazy, and not living up to their potential. They didn't believe they were very intelligent, and didn't feel like they belonged. They lacked a parent in their life who was curious about what was happening underneath and didn't stop until they truly understood it.

GRACE AND ALLEN'S FEAR FOR AN OLDER SON

Grace and Allen are executives in different industries with four kids. Their oldest son is in his late twenties and was diagnosed with anxiety. They believe he has some learning disability but has not been evaluated. He dropped out of college and hasn't been able to hold a job for more than a few months. Most of the jobs he has gotten have been due to his parents' network. He always talks about not feeling smart enough to be there and that he only got the job because of a favor. He smokes a lot of marijuana and has stopped taking his prescribed medication for his anxiety. He spends a significant amount of time in his room and has pulled away from them because he feels like he is always questioned about what he's doing and his plans for his future. She has begun to think that their son is not "lazy" but is dealing with the self-sabotage cycle of impostor syndrome, which may have been for a very long time. Grace wants to have a conversation with her son about this, but she's not sure how. One morning, when he comes down for coffee, Grace engages him in a conversation and starts it with an apology for calling him "lazy" and asks him what is going on. He is startled by the apology and his mom's vulnerability, and he cautiously starts to share his insecurities, deep depression, and feeling like he is an embarrassment to the family. He shares some anger, which is hard for Grace to swallow, but she listens and reflects back what she hears from him. Sometimes, these situations are very complicated and you can feel like you know exactly what's going on, but if something is still not right, and they need greater help, the curiosity and openness to listen to everything and anything can be helpful in figuring out what might bring about positive change.

NAVIGATING SOCIAL ANXIETY AND SHYNESS

Social anxiety can make it challenging to initiate and maintain relationships. These feelings often stem from fear of rejection, embarrassment, or being judged by peers. As a parent, it's important to recognize your child's fears and concerns and provide support. Help them take small steps in pushing their skills forward as they gain greater confidence and the anxiety is reduced. This might include arranging playdates with familiar peers, encouraging participation in small group activities, or role-playing social scenarios at home. Celebrating small successes and providing positive reinforcement can also boost their confidence and willingness to engage socially. Also, a social skills group can be a great contained setting where children are given the opportunity to practice interpersonal skills with a therapist to support the learning process.

DEALING WITH BULLYING AND PEER REJECTION

Bullying and peer rejection are significant barriers to community development for children, and many adults who struggle with impostor syndrome have a history of not belonging. These experiences can lead to feelings of isolation, low self-esteem, distrust, and a reluctance to participate in group activities or connect with any type of group in general. Open and supportive engagement helps your child feel comfortable discussing their social experiences, even when they are negative, complex, or confusing. If bullying is occurring, it's crucial to address it promptly by communicating with the school or relevant authorities, providing emotional support to the child, including therapy, and teaching them coping strategies. Seek to coordinate efforts to address the situation proactively. Do not ignore it as normal. Encouraging involvement in alternative, safe social circles, such as clubs or teams in their interest areas with excellent adult supervision, can also help children find a supportive peer group.

RECIPROCITY AND RUPTURE IN CHILDREN'S RELATIONSHIPS

Reciprocity is vital for children's social development as it teaches them the importance of mutual give-and-take in relationships. It is especially important for two vital reasons in preventing children from developing impostor syndrome: 1. Those with impostor syndrome often over-function in relationships where they feel, or actually are, being evaluated and 2. They can be quick to end or distance themselves from relationships where they have felt vulnerable but have not been supported in the ways that they have wanted.

By engaging in reciprocal interactions, children learn to both give and receive support, kindness, and respect. For instance, when children share toys or help a friend, they experience the benefits of mutual support and cooperation. This process helps them understand the importance of collaboration, laying the groundwork for healthy, balanced relationships and ensuring that the relationships are mutually beneficial. Further, positive experiences with reciprocity build self-esteem and social confidence, as children recognize their ability to contribute meaningfully to their relationships.[27]

---

27 Mallory A. Harris and Ulrich Orth, "The Link Between Self-Esteem and Social Relationships: A Meta-Analysis of Longitudinal Studies," *Journal of Personality and Social Psychology* 119, no. 6 (2020): 1459-1477, doi:10.1037/pspp0000265; Rachel Maunder and Claire P. Monks, "Friendships in Middle Childhood: Links to Peer and School Identification, and General Self-Worth," *The British Journal of Developmental Psychology* 37, no. 2 (2019): 211-29, doi:10.1111/bjdp.12268.

When "over-functioning" in a relationship (i.e., functioning beyond what typically should be expected) , there's a tendency to over-compensate and do more, overvaluing the other person. This leaves the relationship very uneven, and often, the over-functioning person is exhausted, feeling like the relationship gives them very little except for the evaluation component. In these relationships, a child is often seeking approval in return for their dedication and giving. Teach your child how to evaluate how much they give in a relationship and when to set boundaries. Help them to understand why they feel the need to give so much in relationships, and why being seen in a positive light is also crucial. It's important to explore if they are feeling inadequate as themselves, not receiving from others or in a followership rather than leadership position. Stay curious and patient to understand the behavior and to help them reshape into something healthier and relatively even.

UNDERSTANDING RUPTURE IN CHILDREN'S SOCIAL INTERACTIONS

Ruptures in relationships, such as conflicts or disagreements, are natural parts of social interaction. These moments of tension or misunderstanding can be distressing, but they are essential for learning how to navigate complex social dynamics. For example, a disagreement between friends over a game can lead to feelings of frustration or sadness. While these ruptures can challenge children's sense of security, they also present opportunities for growth. Addressing these conflicts helps children develop resilience and problem-solving skills, which are essential for maintaining healthy relationships throughout their lives.

The process of repair following a rupture is crucial for teaching children how to restore and strengthen their relationships. Repair involves recognizing the issue, apologizing if necessary, and working together to resolve the conflict. This might mean talking through feelings, acknowledging mistakes, and finding solutions to prevent future issues. Effective repair not only resolves the immediate problem but also reinforces trust, mutual respect, and a new agreement or way forward in the relationship. This process teaches children the value of accountability and forgiveness, helping them understand that relationships can be mended and strengthened even after difficulties.

Facilitating repair in children's relationships involves guiding them through several key steps: identifying the problem, expressing feelings, and finding a solution. Parents and caregivers can support this process by encouraging open communication, validating children's emotions, and walking them through these steps. For instance, if two friends have a falling out, guiding them to express how they feel and having them listen to each other's perspective helps in understanding and in finding a resolution. Encourage children to offer sincere apologies and make amends where appropriate reinforces the importance of taking responsibility and showing empathy.

Experiencing and addressing conflicts helps children build resilience, teaching them how to handle challenges constructively. When children successfully navigate ruptures and repairs, they develop confidence in their ability to manage interpersonal issues. This resilience is crucial for their overall emotional and social development, as it prepares them to face future conflicts with a constructive mindset. By learning that conflicts can be resolved and relationships can be repaired, children gain a sense of security and competence in their social interactions.

The processes of reciprocity, rupture, and repair significantly contribute to children's emotional intelligence and empathy and make them less reliant on overpleasing to satisfy relationships. Through these experiences, children learn to recognize and manage their own emotions, understand the feelings of others, and respond with empathy. For instance, repairing a relationship after a conflict helps children appreciate different perspectives and the impact of their actions on others. These skills are foundational in the development of healthy relationships with social complexities, from friendships to family dynamics.

Ultimately, the principles of reciprocity, rupture, and repair help children develop positive social skills and maintain healthy relationships. By practicing these principles, children can begin to work on building trust, communicating effectively, and addressing conflicts with a methodology. These skills not only enhance their current relationships but also prepare them for future interactions in school, work, and beyond. Encouraging children to engage in reciprocal interactions, address conflicts constructively, and repair relationships fosters a strong foundation for their social development and well-being, leading to more fulfilling and balanced relationships throughout their lives.

KEY TAKEAWAYS

- **Impostor Syndrome and Social Isolation:** People with impostor syndrome often struggle with social isolation, tending to handle problems alone due to a childhood history of feeling unsupported or dismissed when they needed help. This can lead to difficulties in collaboration and a tendency to overwork.
- **Community-Building as a Counter to Impostor Syndrome:** Engaging in community activities helps children understand the value of collaboration and mutual support, which can counteract the isolating effects of impostor syndrome. This participation helps them see success as a collective effort, not just individual achievement.
- **Vulnerability in Relationships:** Teach your children to be open about their struggles, and validate their feelings. This helps prevent the development of impostor syndrome by showing them that they can be successful and still have vulnerabilities, which are normal and accepted.
- **Social Anxiety:** Addressing social anxiety in children is important for their social development. Gradually expose them to social situations, positive reinforcement, and social skills training to help them build confidence and improve their ability to connect with others.
- **Bullying and Peer Rejection:** Bullying and peer rejection can lead to feelings of isolation and low self-

esteem, which may contribute to the development of impostor syndrome. Address these issues early and provide a supportive environment.

- **Reciprocity in Relationships:** Teach children about reciprocity. The give and take in relationships helps them build healthy, balanced relationships. This understanding can prevent them from overcompensating in relationships where they feel evaluated, which is common in those with impostor syndrome.
- **Rupture and Repair in Social Interactions:** Conflicts or disagreements in relationships, known as ruptures, are natural. Children should learn how to navigate and repair these ruptures to develop resilience and maintain healthy relationships.
- **Role of Parents in Emotional Support:** You play a crucial role in helping children navigate social challenges, such as conflicts or feelings of inadequacy. Providing emotional support, encouraging open communication, and being curious about underlying issues can help children develop a strong sense of self and community.

Conclusion

EMBRACING THE JOURNEY TO GREATNESS

When we wrote our first book, *Own Your Greatness*, which focused on how to defeat impostor syndrome, many supportive readers consistently asked us to consider writing a parenting book on how to prevent impostor syndrome in children. After writing our second book, *Your Unstoppable Greatness*, aimed at helping individuals conquer impostor syndrome should it reemerge and preventing toxic work cultures from triggering it, we realized it was the perfect transition to write *Your Child's Greatness*.

We know that being a parent, while immensely rewarding, can also be very stressful and overwhelming. In 2024, the US Surgeon General issued an advisory on addressing the mental health challenges of parents and caregivers. In this current competitive landscape, where children feel endlessly overscheduled, face constant social media pressures, are increasing lonely, and where admission to the best schools seems elusive, parenting can feel even more challenging. Like many other parents, you may be worried about your child's overall mental health while also wanting them to excel academically and in their extracurricular pursuits.

With *Your Child's Greatness*, we wanted to create a powerful resource to help parents ensure they don't cultivate impostor syndrome in their children. Through the 3 B's model—Belonging, Blooming, and Being—we aim to address common parenting concerns like identity development, family dynamics, reducing performance anxiety, helping children form healthy relationships, managing failure, internalizing success, and creating supportive communities.

REFLECTING ON THE PATH OF PARENTHOOD

When we first became parents, we found ourselves facing countless unexpected challenges as we raised our daughter. Then, with the arrival of our second daughter, it became even clearer that parenting is a lifelong learning process. Watching them grow into strong, competitive athletes has given us a unique perspective on raising healthy, well-adjusted, and impostor-syndrome-free children. We've learned that parenting is not about having all the answers but about continuously adapting, supporting, and encouraging our children as they navigate the world.

Just as our children grow, so does our approach as parents. We recognize that parenting is an ongoing journey of self-discovery, where each phase of our children's lives calls for a new way of showing up for them. And it's a journey that we're grateful to share with you through this book.

USING YOUR CHILD'S GREATNESS ACROSS ALL STAGES OF DEVELOPMENT

We are honored that you have chosen to take this journey with us, and we hope that *Your Child's Greatness* becomes a tool you return to throughout your child's development. From early childhood to adolescence and into adulthood, each stage presents unique opportunities to apply the 3 B's model. The model encourages children to find a sense of belonging, bloom to their fullest potential, and embrace their authentic selves. By keeping these values at the forefront, you are equipping your child with a strong foundation for navigating life's challenges and cultivating a sense of true self-worth.

As parents, it's natural to worry about how our children will face the world and overcome obstacles. Our goal with this book was to give you tools and insights that bring confidence not only to your children but also to you as a parent. Embracing the principles of Belonging, Blooming, and Being will help foster a nurturing and supportive family environment that allows everyone to thrive.

THRIVING TOGETHER: A FAMILY'S PATH TO GREATNESS

We believe that by adopting the 3 B's strategy, you empower your child to own their greatness, thereby reducing your parental stress and strengthening the entire family. Parenting is a partnership that evolves with each new day, experience, and milestone. By supporting your child's growth, you are also fostering your own growth as a parent. It is a journey that calls for compassion, patience, and commitment—not just to our children, but to ourselves.

Thank you for allowing us to be part of your parenting journey. We hope that this book has provided guidance and insight, and that it will continue to serve as a trusted companion. Parenting, at its heart, is about creating a legacy of love, resilience, and authenticity that your children will carry forward into their lives.

Remember, greatness lies in every child, and with your support, they will rise to meet their fullest potential.

GROWING AS A PARENT: EMBRACING LIFELONG LEARNING

As parents, we embark on a path of continual growth and transformation. Each stage of our children's lives brings fresh experiences, challenges, and revelations. We often learn as much from our children as they learn from us, especially as we see the world through their eyes. When we give ourselves the grace to grow alongside them, parenting becomes a journey of personal fulfillment as much as it is about guiding our children. It's a process of learning to let go, to trust in the foundation we've laid, and to appreciate the individuality of each child.

Throughout *Your Child's Greatness*, we have provided tools to help you support your child's development without instilling impostor syndrome. However, there is no one-size-fits-all approach to parenting, and every family will navigate this path differently. What matters most is your commitment to fostering a nurturing, encouraging, and supportive environment, one in which both you and your child can thrive.

By embracing this journey of lifelong learning, you model resilience and adaptability, teaching your children the value of self-improvement and self-compassion. These qualities will not only serve you as a parent but will also become invaluable skills that your children can draw upon throughout their own lives.

THE IMPACT OF COMMUNITY: BUILDING A SUPPORTIVE NETWORK

Parenting does not happen in isolation; it takes a community. The challenges of raising children are made more manageable—and more joyful—when we have a network of family, friends, educators, and mentors who share our values and support our efforts. In an era where digital connections are plentiful yet meaningful relationships can sometimes feel scarce, building a supportive community has never been more important.

As you continue your journey, consider seeking out like-minded parents who share a commitment to fostering self-worth and resilience in their children. These connections can provide you with fresh perspectives, mutual encouragement, and a sense of solidarity as you navigate parenting challenges. Additionally, sharing your experiences and insights from *Your Child's Greatness* can reinforce these principles in your community, creating a ripple effect that benefits everyone involved.

Through such a network, your child will also find mentors and friends who reinforce the values of Belonging, Blooming, and Being. Children learn by observing, and seeing their parents form healthy, supportive connections helps them understand the importance of surrounding themselves with people who encourage them to grow and embrace their authentic selves.

MOVING FORWARD WITH CONFIDENCE AND PURPOSE

Parenting is one of life's greatest and most rewarding responsibilities. At times, it may seem overwhelming, and the stakes can feel high. But know that the effort you put into understanding, supporting, and nurturing your child's unique greatness is invaluable. As you move forward, we encourage you to embrace each day with the confidence that you are making a difference, even in moments when the results may not be immediately visible.

Your commitment to raising a well-adjusted, confident, and compassionate individual will have a profound impact—not just on your child but on all those they encounter. Through *Your Child's Greatness*, you have equipped yourself with a powerful toolkit for fostering a sense of belonging, resilience, and purpose within your family.

We are honored to be part of your journey, and we believe that by continuing to cultivate these qualities, you will help your child, and yourself, discover and celebrate true greatness. Thank you for letting us walk alongside you on this journey, and remember that each step you take toward intentional, mindful parenting brings you closer to the thriving family life you envision.

This concludes our book, but it's only the beginning of a powerful and rewarding path. We hope that *Your Child's Greatness* will remain a treasured resource that you revisit at every stage, reminding you of the incredible impact you have as a parent. In nurturing your child's greatness, you are indeed nurturing your own, and together, your family will flourish. We hope that you have been inspired to consciously consider how you want to raise your children and the legacy of self-worth, confidence, and resilience you want to instill in them.

BIBLIOGRAPHY

Allen, Joseph P., Stuart T. Hauser, Kathy L. Bell, and Thomas G. O'Connor. "Longitudinal Assessment of Autonomy and Relatedness in Adolescent-Family Interactions as Predictors of Adolescent Ego Development and Self-Esteem." *Child Development* 65, no. 1 (1994): 179–94.

American Psychiatric Association. *Diagnostic and Statistical Manual of Mental Disorders*. 5th ed. Arlington, VA: American Psychiatric Association, 2013.

American Psychiatric Association. *Diagnostic and Statistical Manual of Mental Disorders: DSM-5-TR*. 5th ed., text rev. Washington, DC: American Psychiatric Association, 2022. "Attention-Deficit/Hyperactivity Disorder," 59–66.

American Psychiatric Association. *Diagnostic and Statistical Manual of Mental Disorders: DSM-5-TR*. 5th ed., text rev. Washington, DC: American Psychiatric Association, 2022. "Autism Spectrum Disorder," 53–58.

American Psychological Association Dictionary of Psychology. "Emotional Regulation." dictionary.apa.org/emotion-regulation. Accessed March 19, 2024.

American Psychological Association Dictionary of Psychology. "Performance Anxiety." dictionary.apa.org/performance-anxiety. Accessed March 12, 2024.

American Psychological Association Dictionary of Psychology. "Self-Talk." https://dictionary.apa.org/self-talk. Accessed May 29, 2024.

Cambridge Learner's Dictionary. "Self-Esteem." Accessed June 15, 2024. https://dictionary.cambridge.org/us/dictionary/learner-english/self-esteem. Accessed June 15, 2024.

Curran, T., and A. Hill. "Perfectionism Is Increasing Over Time: A Meta-Analysis of Birth Cohort Differences from 1989 to 2016." *Psychological Bulletin* 145, no. 4 (2019): 410–29. https://doi.org/10.1037/bul0000138.

Callaghan, Thomas et al. "The Relationships between Perfectionism and Symptoms of Depression, Anxiety, and Obsessive-Compulsive Disorder in Adults: A Systematic Review and Meta-Analysis." *Cognitive Behaviour Therapy* 53, no. 2 (2024): 121–32. https://doi.org/10.1080/16506073.2023.2277121.

Gardner, Howard. *Frames of Mind: The Theory of Multiple Intelligences*. New York: Basic Books, 1983.

Greater Good Science Center. "Mindfulness Definition," *Greater Good Magazine*. Accessed May 29, 2024. https://greatergood.berkeley.edu/topic/mindfulness/definition.

Handley, A. et al. "The Relationships between Perfectionism, Pathological Worry and Generalised Anxiety Disorder." *BMC Psychiatry* 14 (2014): 98. https://doi.org/10.1186/1471-244X-14-98.

Harris, Mallory A., and Ulrich Orth. "The Link Between Self-Esteem and Social Relationships: A Meta-Analysis of Longitudinal Studies." *Journal of Personality and Social Psychology* 119, no. 6 (2020): 1459–477.

Hendricks, B., T. Werner, L. Shipway, and G. J. Turinetti. "Recidivism among Spousal Abusers: Predictions and Program Evaluation." *Journal of Interpersonal Violence* 21, no. 6 (2006): 703–16.

Hewitt, P., and G. Flett. "Perfectionism in the Self and Social Context: Conceptualization, Assessment, and Association with Psychopathology." *Journal of Personality and Social Psychology* 60, no. 3 (March 1991): 456–70. https://doi.org/10.1037/0022-3514.60.3.456.

Lee, Linda E. et al. "Perfectionism and the Impostor Phenomenon in Academically Talented Undergraduates." *Gifted Child Quarterly* 65, no. 3 (2021): 220–34. https://doi.org/10.1177/0016986220969396.

Luque-Suárez, Mónica et al. "Promoting Emotional and Social Well-Being and a Sense of Belonging in Adolescents through Participation in Volunteering." *Healthcare* 9, no. 3 (March 22, 2021): 359.

Ma, Chunhua, Yongfeng Ma, and Youpeng Wang. "Parental Autonomy Support and Mental Health among Chinese Adolescents and Emerging Adults: The Mediating Role of Self-Esteem." *International Journal of Environmental Research and Public Health* 19, no. 21 (2022): 14029.

Maunder, Rachel, and Claire P Monks. "Friendships in Middle Childhood: Links to Peer and School Identification, and General Self-Worth." *The British Journal of Developmental Psychology* 37, no. 2 (2019): 211–29.

Merriam-Webster Dictionary. "Failure." Accessed August 2, 2024. https://www.merriam-webster.com/dictionary/failure.

Merriam-Webster Dictionary. "Self-Worth." Accessed June 15, 2024.

Mousavi, S., and A. F. Meshkini. "Effect of Mental Imagery upon the Reduction of Athletes Anxiety during Sport Performance." *International Journal of Academic Research in Business and Social Sciences* 1, no. 3 (2011): 97–108.

Pérez-Fuentes, María del Carmen, et al. "Parenting Practices, Life Satisfaction, and the Role of Self-Esteem in Adolescents." *International Journal of Environmental Research and Public Health* 16, no. 20 (2019): 4045. doi:10.3390/ijerph16204045.

Ruchika, Shaurya Prakash. "Mindfulness Meditation: Impact on Attentional Control and Emotion Dysregulation." *Archives of Clinical Neuropsychology* 36, no. 7 (October 2021): 1283–90.

Slutzky, Carly B., and Sandra D. Simpkins. "The Link Between Children's Sport Participation and Self-Esteem: Exploring the Mediating Role of Sport Self-Concept." *Psychology of Sport and Exercise* 10, no. 3 (2009): 381–89.

Thomas, K. W., and Kilmann, R. H. "Thomas-Kilmann Conflict Mode Instrument." *Group & Organization Management* 1, no. 2: 249–51.

Villwock, Jennifer A. et al. "Impostor Syndrome and Burnout among American Medical Students: A Pilot Study." *International Journal of Medical Education* 7 (2016): 364–69.

Wang, Y. et al. "The Relationship between Perfectionism and Social Anxiety: A Moderated Mediation Model." *International Journal of Environmental Research and Public Health* 19, no. 19 (2022): 12934. https://doi.org/10.3390/ijerph191912934.

Wu R. et al. "Brief Mindfulness Meditation Improves Emotion Processing." *Frontiers in Neuroscience* 13 (2019): 1074. https://doi.org/10.3389/fnins.2019.01074.

Zahari, Jaafa, and Mohar Kassim R. "The Effectiveness of Imagery Training on Anxiety Levels and Performance amongst Athletes in Archery." *Australian Journal of Basic and Applied Sciences* 10, no. 11 (2016): 207–13.

ACKNOWLEDGMENTS

First and foremost, we would like to thank our parents, Guy, Marguerite, Anna, and Francisco. Thank you for being the best parents anyone could ask for, even with the humanity of it all—mistakes, missteps, and mishaps included. We are grateful for all the opportunities you created for us while still having to learn a new language, grapple with generational patterns you were trying to break, and trying to survive and thrive as immigrants in America. You are our heroes, and we are awestruck by your resilience, love, strength, and dedication to being the best parents you could be. We appreciate all you have given to us, sacrificed for us, and been through with us. We hope to be as incredible of parents to our children, as you were to us. Thank you for your love and continuing encouragement. You are our inspiration and role models.

We would like to thank our children, Nia and Maya, who have been the most patient, supportive, and kind companions during this book journey. It has been amazing to watch you grow into young women from the first book until now. You are such thoughtful, kind, and funny people, and we love that we get to share this life with you. We so admire your strength, determination, humor, and deep love you give to us. You are our light, and we hope we are the parents you so deserve, as we strive to be better every day.

We would also like to thank our siblings Galia, Anna Maria, Cristina, and our brother-in-law Rodney. We appreciate the lessons you have given us about raising children and the special care you have given to our children. We know that it indeed takes a village to raise a child. Thank you for all your support over the years.

Thank you to all the parents, coaches, amazing mentors, and athletes that we have met through fencing. Thank you for inspiring perseverance, resilience, community, and laughs when it's super hard to remember why we are engaged in this wacky sport.

A special thank you to Peter Westbrook, a six-time Olympic fencer and founder of the Peter Westbrook Foundation (PWF), who passed days before we finished this book. Getting to know you and to share seminal moments in our lives together has been the deepest honor. Thank you for being a "parent" to so many children who needed your guidance, your unfailing belief in them, and your ability to appreciate the beauty of a flawed human. You introduced our family to a sport that our children fell in love with and that has brought us all so much learning that will continue much longer than we can imagine. Thank you for showing us what true community looks like and what it means to belong to something bigger. You built a beautiful family that will sustain your legacy and get ever stronger. Peter used to always say that PWF doesn't only build Olympians, that more importantly it builds Olympians in life, and we will continue to strive to live up to that mission.

To our friends and colleagues, too numerous to mention, who gave us parenting tips, best practices, and just an open ear as we started our parental journey, we will never forget your kindness and how you took the time to give advice to us, even when you may have been overwhelmed with your own parental responsibilities. Thank you.

To our clients, who have allowed us to be with them and support them through their parenting journeys, it is a joy to watch you parent with love and vulnerability—trying to break generational patterns and offer something different and more to your children. You never let fear be the guide. You sit outside your comfort zone regularly, challenge yourself to try new things that feel scary, and defy authority around how your kids should behave and be in the world. We are so proud of you for raising a confident and resilient next generation.

Thank you to our readers. You have trusted us to be a guide to your process in dealing with the origins of feeling like a fraud and have fought back the idea that there is nothing you can do about it. You know better and you want better for your children and the generations that follow. Kudos to you for forever believing that we can do better and appreciate who we are at the same time!

And finally, we would like to acknowledge and express gratitude to our ancestors (especially Aunt Jeanette) and to all who have provided care to us and to our children. We have learned so much from your tenderness, your wisdom, and the warmth you demonstrate in your everyday connection to children. It is through your wonderful strength and resilience that we were able to bring the words to life in this book. We are so grateful for your guidance and continue to learn from your example to be the best parents and caregivers possible.

ABOUT THE AUTHORS

Dr. Lisa Orbé-Austin is a licensed psychologist and executive coach. She earned her doctorate in counseling psychology from Columbia University. Her expertise on impostor syndrome is regularly sought by the media, and she has appeared in outlets such as *Financial Times*, the *Today Show*, *Good Morning America*, *Forbes*, *Huffington Post*, and *Refinery29*. She has also been honored twice as a Top Voice on LinkedIn in the areas of Job Search and Careers and Mental Health. Dr. Orbé-Austin has been an invited speaker at various national conferences. She recently gave a TEDx talk entitled "The Impostor Syndrome Paradox: Unleashing the Power of You."

Trained as a clinician and researcher, her work is focused on providing practical, achievable results through research-backed science. She is a contributor to The American Psychological Association's volume on Imposter Phenomenon entitled *The Impostor Phenomenon: Psychological Research, Theory, and Interventions* (APA Press, 2024).

Her first book, *Own Your Greatness: Overcome Impostor Syndrome, Beat Self-Doubt, and Succeed in Life* (Ulysses Press, 2020), coauthored with her partner, Dr. Richard Orbé-Austin, was released in April 2020. Their book was a finalist for the Foreword INDIES Book Award. Her second book, *Your Unstoppable Greatness: Break Free of Impostor Syndrome, Cultivate Your Agency, and Achieve Your Ultimate Career Goals* (Ulysses Press, 2022) is focused on dealing with the systemic dynamics in workplaces and cultures that keep impostor syndrome in place and how to directly combat those dynamics.

Dr. Richard Orbé-Austin is a licensed psychologist, executive coach, and consultant. He earned his PhD in counseling psychology from Fordham University's Graduate School of Education and his BA in psychology from NYU. In his practice, Dr. Orbé-Austin works with executives, senior leaders, and mid-career professionals to overcome impostor syndrome, identify their best-fit career options, advance their career goals, and strengthen their leadership skills. He also regularly consults to academic institutions, corporations, and nonprofit organizations on issues related to leadership, diversity, equity and inclusion, anti-racist practice, burnout prevention, impostor syndrome, and creating healthy workplaces.

Dr. Orbé-Austin's opinions and writings have appeared in a variety of publications and academic journals, including *Forbes, Fast Company, ThriveGlobal, Diversity Executive*, the *Journal of Multicultural Counseling & Development*, and the *Handbook of Racial-Cultural Counseling and Psychology*. He is a TEDx speaker and the author of the book *Own Your Greatness: Overcome Impostor Syndrome, Beat Self-Doubt, and Succeed in Life* (Ulysses Press, 2020), coauthored with his partner, Dr. Lisa Orbé-Austin. The goal of the book is to provide a systematic formula to eliminate impostor syndrome and to assist readers to own their talents and power in order to fully realize their goals and lead a more balanced life. It was a Foreword INDIES Book Award Finalist. His second book *Your Unstoppable Greatness: Break Free from Impostor Syndrome, Cultivate Your Agency, and Achieve Your Ultimate Career Goals* (Ulysses Press, December 2022), also coauthored with his partner, focuses on how to sustain your impostor syndrome–free life, reduce burnout, and improve healthy leadership skills while conquering toxic work cultures. He is also a contributor to the American Psychological Association's volume on impostor phenomenon, entitled *The Impostor Phenomenon: Psychological Research, Theory, and Interventions* (APA Press, March 2024).

OTHER BOOKS FROM LISA & RICHARD ORBÉ-AUSTIN

ALSO AVAILABLE FROM ULYSSES PRESS

visit www.ulyssespress.com for more information